Annotated Legal Documents on Islam in Europe: Portugal

Annotated Legal Documents on Islam in Europe

VOLUME 19

The titles published in this series are listed at *brill.com/ldie*

Annotated Legal Documents on Islam in Europe

Portugal

Compiled, Annotated and Authored by

Jónatas E.M. Machado
(*Univ Coimbra, University of Coimbra Institute of Legal Research, Faculty of Law*)

Sofia Caseiro
(*School of Education and Social Sciences, Polytechnic of Leiria*)

BRILL

LEIDEN | BOSTON

Library of Congress Cataloging-in-Publication Data

Names: Machado, Jónatas Eduardo Mendes, complier, writer of annotation, author. | Caseiro, Sofia, compiler, writer of annotation, author.
Title: Annotated legal documents on Islam in Europe. Portugal / compiled, annotated, and authored by Jónatas E.M. Machado, Sofia Caseiro.
Description: Leiden, the Netherlands : Koninklijke Brill NV, [2020] | Series: Annotated legal documents on Islam in Europe, 2214-1340 ; volume 19 | Includes bibliographical references and index.
Identifiers: LCCN 2020045238 | ISBN 9789004444553 (paperback)
Subjects: LCSH: Muslims–Legal status, laws, etc.–Portugal.
Classification: LCC KKQ2467.M56 M33 2020 | DDC 342.46908/5297–dc23
LC record available at https://lccn.loc.gov/2020045238

Typeface for the Latin, Greek, and Cyrillic scripts: "Brill". See and download: brill.com/brill-typeface.

ISSN 2214-1340
ISBN 978-90-04-44455-3 (paperback)

This book is printed on acid-free paper and produced in a sustainable manner.

Contents

Foreword by the Editors

This is the nineteenth volume in the series *Annotated Legal Documents on Islam in Europe*. The publication of this series responds to the widespread lack of sound information about the legal status of Islam in Europe. In principle, this information is easily available to those who are willing to make the effort and know enough about the subject to ask the right questions of the digital search engines. But that requires both expertise and effort, and it takes place in an environment where the public political debate on Islam in many European countries is characterised by increasing concern and fear. Islam has come to be broadly perceived as a security issue rather than a religion like others in Europe. But the concern has also moved into the legal field, most markedly, of course, with discussions about limitations on Muslim female dress being enacted in a growing number of countries, or the ban on building minarets on mosques in Switzerland, or restrictions on building mosques in certain Austrian provinces. At the same time, in a number of European states like Austria and Germany, legislation is enacted and state treaties are negotiated which aim to establish a stable and reliable basis for Muslim life and organisation. Even so, such measures are under scrutiny by an increasingly sceptical European public, sometimes ignoring the legal principles of secularity, not least the demands of state neutrality towards and equal treatment of all religions and beliefs regardless of numbers of adherents or public reputation.

In addition, the religious status and rights of Muslims in the various European countries differ significantly, due to different historical developments regarding the organisation of the relations between the state and religions. Furthermore, while in some states laws regulating such matters introduced decades ago are still in force and have to be re-interpreted in the face of a 'newcomer' religion, others have introduced new laws that consider the increasing religious plurality within Europe. Despite the common legal and political foundations constructed since 1945 in instruments such as the European Convention on Human Rights and the more recently accumulated legislation of the European Union, this closer look reveals remarkable differences due to the extent of separating state and religion or establishing co-operative structures. In some countries Islam has an officially recognised status which in some cases originated in the first half of the 20th century. In other countries no such recognition of any religion is available even if informal ways of favouring one religion over another may exist. Since 1990 especially, European courts have moved to equalise the status of Islam with that of other religions in the practical exercise of religious freedom in various countries. Particular practices regarded as core religious obligations—in the case of Muslims dress codes and practices such as male circumcision, access to correctly slaughtered meat and otherwise *halal* food, free time for the main periods of worship and religious festivals, and the right to build mosques—can be controversial in some countries while less so in others. In the course of the ongoing process of self-organisation and the participation of Muslims in civil societies and their co-operation with the state, children's access to Islamic religious instruction or the education of Muslim theologians can be achieved in co-operation with the state education systems in some countries, while in others the community must rely on its own arrangements. The practically pressing issue of financing the religious infrastructure is still far from being settled in many countries.

The aim of this series is to make this legislation available to both the interested researcher and the practising lawyer. Altogether the series is expected to comprise 32 volumes, one for each of the 27 countries of the European Union plus Norway, Switzerland and the United Kingdom and a volume each dealing with the European Union (treaties, directives and decisions of the Court of Justice of the European Communities) and the European Court of Human Rights. Excerpts of relevant legislation are introduced and summarised by the volume compiler, and where court cases have provided significant interpretation of the law they will also be referred to. The legislation itself is reproduced in the original language, as the editors and the publisher agreed early on in the preparation of the series that any attempt to translate legislation into English would be unsatisfactory and risked being misleading. The comments and analysis by the author should give sufficient guidance to users to allow a decision as to whether to arrange a translation for their specific purposes.

While there is in many countries legislation explicitly referring to aspects of Islam, most often regarding official recognition or to do with education, in other countries there is none. With the exception of a formal agreement with the Ismaili community, Portugal has no legislation specifically dealing with Islam. Islamic communities, some of which are well-established, can be included within various categories of religious association on equal terms with other religious communities. Only the Catholic church retains some of the regulation inherited from concordats with Rome.

An attempt has been made to ensure that the volumes are structured in as similar a manner as possible. The starting point for this has been the thematic organisation used variously in the *Yearbook of Muslims in Europe* which Brill has published annually since 2009. But it has been only a starting point, and in each volume the compiler and the editors have agreed on the structure which makes most sense for the legislation of the country concerned. Normally one member of the editorial group takes responsibility for discussing the structure and compilation of each volume with the compiler. In this instance, this task was undertaken by Prof. Silvio Ferrari. We are also grateful to Kate Elliott for the care shown in copy editing the volume. The initiative for this project came from the publisher, where Nicolette van der Hoek and Nienke Brienen-Moolenaar have played an invaluable role in ensuring that the project has maintained its momentum. As editors, we appreciate how much their expertise contributes to ensuring that a project like this can run smoothly.

It is in the nature of such a project that each volume, if left as it stands, will gradually become out of date as new legislation and cases appear. From 2019 the series has become available online in a format which in due course will permit regular updating.

The Editors
June 2020

Introductory Remarks

Human interpretations of religions played influential roles, positive and negative, in societies along history and cross the globe. Like any authority, that exercised in the name of religion is not immune from abuse.

Combatting global religious intolerance starts at home. Hence the importance of this study on the legal status of Islam in Portugal. The history of Portugal created special links with Muslim traditions and communities. This study confirms at the outset the fact that freedom of religion or belief, along with all universal human rights, derive their impact from being deeply rooted in national constitutional and legislative frameworks.

I fondly remember how much I admired its multi-cultural features when I served as Ambassador of Egypt in Portugal between 2003–2007. At a farewell lunch before my departure, in the spring of 2007, I had the honour of receiving President Jorge Sampaio as a guest of honour. The complex relations between religion and culture and the tension between the enriching and conflictual sides of human diversity were the main topics of our rich discussion, with several Portuguese intellectuals and foreign ambassadors and with a focus on the unique history and geography of Portugal. It was one of those high-quality discussions that remain engraved in intellectual memory, planting seeds for undefined future projects.

We never imagined during this lunch that President Sampaio and I would meet again a few months later in two different capacities to collaborate on the same topic of religion, rights and diversity! President Sampaio as Special Representative of the United Nations for the Dialogue of Civilizations while I was then director of the human rights treaties' division at the United Nations human rights office in Geneva.

From the larger horizon of dialogue among civilizations, our collaboration zoomed on the human rights responsibilities of religious actors. A complex topic given the reciprocal doubts between the two disciplines, the requirements of secularism and related politics and polarisation. I was coordinating at that time an initiative by the Office of the High Commissioner for Human Rights (OHCHR) that focused on one aspect of the problem of religions and rights: hate speech. Is freedom of religion at odds with freedom of expression? Where is the demarcation line between free speech and hate speech? What are the responsibilities of religious actors in this area?

It took us between 2008 and 2012 to provide answers to these questions. "Us", being a consortium of independent human rights mechanisms and experts from within the United Nations system and the civil society, including its religious sphere. This initiative resulted in the adoption of the Rabat Plan of Action against incitement to hatred. This plan defined the responsibilities of religious leaders, among other actors, to prevent and remedy to hate speech in the name of their beliefs. The research process launched by OHCHR consisted of mapping legislative approaches, public policies, and case law in different regions regarding the definition of and combatting hate speech that constitutes incitement to violence or discrimination, as per article 20 of the International Covenant on Civil and Political Rights of 1976. President Sampaio inaugurated the European consultation, which was the first among all regional consultations, held in Vienna in February 2011. He also co-chaired with Navy Pillay, the High Commissioner for Human Rights at that time, the panel of experts that launched the Rabat Plan of action in Geneva in November 2011. Since then, the Rabat criteria on hate speech became widely known and usefully implemented. The need to transcend legal debates and inter-faith dialogues into action increases as our societies become more multi-religious and multi-cultural than ever. This explains why this tool of fighting incitement to hatred has been translated into 32 languages already.[1]

The efforts of the United Nations human rights office to defend freedom of religion or belief as well as the rights of all minorities, including religious minorities, are a central part of the mandate of the High Commissioner for Human Rights, as well as human rights independent expert mechanisms established by states. Rights also come with responsibilities. While states bear the primary responsibility in the promotion and protection of human rights, non-state actors also bear human rights responsibilities, including faith actors.

The Rabat standards on hate speech prompted further development of the content of human rights responsibilities of faith actors. While the Rabat Plan of Action mentions "religious leaders", the Beirut declaration and its corresponding 18 Commitments on Faith for Rights of 2017 addresses "faith based actors", which is an enlargement in scope. This expert-led new set of standards also widens the scope of human rights responsibilities of faith actors, beyond hate speech, into the full spectrum of human rights. The Faith for Rights framework of 2017 is a living document that provides a shared narrative, comprehensible for both rights and faith communities. OHCHR spearheaded an effort that led to creating an innovative peer-to-peer learning tool with a view to empowering advocates, experts and academics to constantly enrich this interdisciplinary approach to the complex but vital interaction between rights and religions.[2]

1 https://www.ohchr.org/EN/NewsEvents/Pages/Hate-speech-threshold-test.aspx.

2 https://www.ohchr.org/EN/NewsEvents/Pages/Faith4Rights_Toolkit.aspx.

As stated by Michael Bachelet, the UN High Commissioner for Human Rights, in April 2019:

> We hope the 'Faith for Rights' framework will also inspire interdisciplinary research on questions related to faith and rights. Deeper exploration of the ethical and spiritual foundations provided by religions and beliefs can help to debunk the myth that human rights are solely Western values. On the contrary: the human rights agenda is rooted in cultures across the world. Respect for human life, and human dignity, wellbeing and justice, are common to us all. 'Faith' can indeed stand up for 'Rights' so that both enhance each other.[3]

This is why this study can contribute to both national and international understanding and progressive development of human rights law.

Dr. Ibrahim Salama
Chief of Human Rights Treaties Branch of the Office of the United Nations (UN) High Commissioner for Human Rights
Former Ambassador of Egypt in Lisbon

3 https://www.ohchr.org/en/NewsEvents/Pages/DisplayNews.aspx?NewsID=24531&LangID=E.

General Introduction

In this work, we are trying to give a brief account of the political, legal and social reality of the various Islamic communities in Portugal. We will have as the main point of reference the Portuguese Constitution of 1976, still in force, the Religious Freedom Act of 2001, the general civil and penal legislation and some special rules on particular aspects of the exercise of religious freedom. Portugal was formed geographically, politically, socially and culturally in the Christian Reconquest and maritime expansion, so the country's cultural identity is inseparable from the influence of Catholicism. Even those who do not profess the Catholic faith will hardly be able to escape from this spiritual and intellectual matrix. At the same time, we cannot ignore that the existing Muslim communities in Portugal have been able to put down roots in the deep soil of the historical presence of Islam in the Iberian Peninsula and the marks, footprints, traces and tracks it has left behind. However, there are two leading ideas or motifs that can explain the current legal regime of religious freedom in Portugal. On the one hand, it must be acknowledged that at the deep root of Roman Catholicism important humanistic and universalist principles can be found, beneficial to a free and open encounter with other peoples and cultures. In these principles there should be no place for the distinction between Jew and Greek, free and slave, or man and woman. On the other hand, we know that history is not just a past. It is also present and future because the past has also been present and future. This means that we do not necessarily have to be stuck with the past even when we build on it. We can learn from past experience and explore new possibilities and alternatives in the present and for the future. The Portuguese free and democratic constitutional order, built throughout on the history of Portugal, asserts itself as a universalist and humanist order where all citizens, regardless of their religious and ideological convictions, can be seen as full members of the political community, with equal dignity, freedom and responsibility. In this regard, the main purpose of the 1976 Portuguese Constitution is for the Islamic community in Portugal proudly to feel and be perceived as an absolutely essential part of the political community and the country's economic, social and cultural reality and destiny.

CHAPTER 1

Status of Religious Communities

1.1 Constitutional Guarantees

The concept of freedom of religion was always viewed with suspicion in a state that had developed its identity out of deep Catholic Christian roots and traditions. Over the centuries, the Catholic Church and the Portuguese monarchs saw themselves as two different sides of the same spiritual coin, working hand in hand in the Crusades, in the Christian reconquest of the Iberian territory and the conquest of new lands and peoples and their conversion to the Christian faith. This historical process was by no means static, but rather a dynamic evolution characterised by dialectical tension, reciprocal influence and permanent theological-political learning and adaptation. Neither the state nor the Church remained unchanged in the face of history.

That common sense of mission notwithstanding, the relationship between the Catholic Church and the Portuguese monarchs was never easy. There were always tensions relating to property, taxes, the nomination of bishops and the temporal authority of the Pope. The tensions intensified as the Church responded to the challenges of the Protestant Reformation that spread throughout northern Europe and potentially also threatened the south, first by monarchical Absolutism, and then by the spread of liberal political ideas. This reality, which characterised the history of Portugal, did not change immediately after the liberal revolution of 1820. The Constitution of 1820, although providing for freedom of thought, expression and the press, established that the Bishops should guarantee, through a special court, respect for religious dogma and morals. One of the main duties of every Portuguese citizen was to venerate religion.

However, the constitutionalism has, since the first Constitutional text in 1822, included a right of private free exercise of religion (*devotio privata*) granted to foreigners. This right was granted largely due to the significant presence, in Lisbon and Porto, of wealthy British and German businessmen mostly linked to the wine production, industry and trade. In the 19th century, the king's powers were legitimised by God. Thus, we can find in each of the monarchical Constitutions of Portugal the provision about the Religion of the state. The official religion was the Roman Catholic Church. As far as foreigners were concerned, a right to freedom of religion was recognised, although no public worship was allowed.[1] This constitution, originally designed to be the Constitution of the United Kingdom of Portugal, Brazil and the Algarves, had only just come into force when Brazil became independent in 1822, and political turmoil followed.

After the Constitutional Charter of 1826, the Roman Catholic Church continued to be the official religion of the state. Article 6 still established freedom of religion for foreigners, as long as the worship was domestic and carried out in a proper house, without the semblance of a place of worship. In parallel, the constitution also included a provision that prohibited persecution on the grounds of religion, when there was no offence to the state and morals.[2] However, Article 145 of the Constitution of 1826 was incompatible with the freedom of Article 6. On the one hand, only foreigners could practise a different religion in a private space, an arrangement which was not allowed to Portuguese citizens. This was a natural concession to the influential foreign communities residing in Portugal, linked to industry and trade, namely the British and the German, where Protestantism was predominant. On the other hand, there was no place for persecution on the grounds of religion if there was no offence to the state. It was understood that it was not possible to be a true Portuguese citizen and not be Catholic, the penalty for the latter being denationalisation. However, also under this law, it was possible for a foreigner to be naturalised, under Article 7 (4), whatever religion they practised. Thus, many naturalised Portuguese citizens could be Portuguese and not Catholic.[3]

The Republican Revolution in 1910 was a decisive moment, not only for religious freedom in Portugal but also for the relations between the different religions and the state.[4] According to prevailing republican doctrine, "the State's mission has nothing to do with ideas of the members of the society". The state was now freed from any religious legitimation and values.[5] Religion was to be seen, primarily, as a matter of individual conscience and conviction.

1 Lopes, Manuela Baptista, "A Liberdade Religiosa em Portugal, a(s) constituição (ões) e o tribunal constitucional", in *Estudos em Homenagem ao Conselheiro Presidente Rui Moura Ramos, Volume 1—Direito Constitucional, Direito Constitucional Europeu, Direito Europeu*, Maria Lúcia Amaral (ed) (Coimbra: Almedina, 2016), pp. 304–305.

2 Torres Gutiérrez, Alejandro, *El derecho de libertad religiosa en Portugal* (Madrid: Editorial Dykinson, 2010), p. 56.

3 Torres Gutiérrez, El derecho, pp. 56–57.

4 Machado, Jónatas E.M., *Liberdade Religiosa numa comunidade constitucional inclusiva dos direitos da verdade aos direitos dos cidadãos* (Coimbra: Coimbra Editora, 1996), p. 115.

5 Machado, *Liberdade Religiosa*, p. 116.

The first republican Constitution of 1911 put an end to the religious aspect of the Constitution,[6] recognising the right to religious freedom only as a purely civil right. This right aims only to oppose intolerance from other citizens and the state and to prevent the public service from interfering in favour of the most widely practised religion.[7] There is a severe fracture in the relationship between state and religion. Republicans feared that the Church would influence society, according to a more conservative and traditionalist orientation, considering its natural hegemony over the public sphere,[8] so measures were taken to suppress the influence of the Church in the public sphere as far as possible.

Following this same logic, the Roman Catholic Church was no longer considered the official religion of the state, and other religions were considered legitimate as long as they did not offend the morals and the principles of the Portuguese state.[9] Religious freedom, as an individual right, was possible only with some significant structural and institutional changes.

The Law of Separation of the State and Churches of 1911 established the freedom of conscience and worship of any religion and religious teaching, and provided sanctions for disturbance of public worship, and offences against ministries of any religion, as a public offence.[10] Portuguese republican political thought is a complex reality. The legal reference to "churches", in the plural, shows that the many Portuguese republicans, among which some Protestant influence could be seen, were still largely thinking within a Christian mindset, taking into consideration the different Christian confessions[11] that had developed in Europe and the United States after the Reformation. At the same time, this reference in the plural was a way of making it clear, in the eyes of the Catholic Church and of all the people, that this particular religious entity was just one among many, without any claim to special status or dignity. In this way, the Catholic Church, which had always played a central and preponderant role in the political and cultural landscape of Portugal, was deliberately harassed and relativised, put in its place, by the dominant political party. Freemason and Jacobin lines of anti-clericalism could also be detected in some republican intellectuals, along with a Catholic perspective, with deep medieval monarchist roots, that emphasised the temporal supremacy of the state over

6 Torres Gutiérrez, *El derecho*, p. 88.

7 Machado, *Liberdade Religiosa*, p. 116.

8 Torres Gutiérrez, *El derecho*, p. 89.

9 Torres Gutiérrez, *El derecho*, p. 90.

10 Lopes, "A Liberdade Religiosa …", p. 311.

11 The term "confessions" is used in Portuguese legislation referring to different religions (Christanity, Budism and Islam, for example) and also to different confessional communities within each religion (Catholics, Ortodoxs and Lutherans, for example).

the Church. This law intensified the confrontation between public power and Catholic hierarchy and the tension in a society in which the majority were religious.[12] As a result of its enactment, the Holy See severed diplomatic relation with the Portuguese state. This law was widely discussed for years, and conflicted with Decree no. 3856 in 1918 that redraws the controversial provisions against the Catholic Church.[13]

The discussion was not settled until 1926, the year in which the first Republic was brought down by a military coup. The so-called New State (Estado Novo) emerged from this coup, leading to a new Constitutional text in 1933. On religious freedom, this new normative framework is equivalent to the original republican constitution: it provides a general right to religious freedom, prohibiting persecution on grounds of religion and the exemption of obligations rooted in religion.[14] The Estado Novo was impregnated by a markedly conservative Catholic ideology. However, it was a highly state-centred and nationalist political reality, still very committed to the exclusivist claims of its colonial rule, therefore highly suspicious of the universalist pretensions of the Holy See and the continuing threats of political interference from the local leadership of the Catholic Church.

The 1933 Constitution went further in establishing freedom for the practice of every form of worship, guaranteeing rights to self-organisation, self-regulation and self-determination, recognising legal personality to every religious community.[15] Formally, the constitution was in perfect harmony with the framework needed for a constitutional and democratic state. However, these freedoms were limited by other provisions, the interpretation and application of which to concrete situations almost instinctively assumed a strong Catholic bias, such as the limitation of the state's sovereignty by confessional moral rules, and entrusting the state to promote religious dogma, defending moral values and perfecting the civic and moral qualities of the citizens.[16]

The 1940 Concordat between the Catholic Church and the Portuguese state recognised the importance of Catholicism in the history and culture of Portugal, mitigating Republican anti-clericalism. However, in establishing the lines governing cooperation between the Catholic Church and the state it does not

12 Assembleia da República, Separação do Estado das Igrejas (1911), available at https://www.parlamento.pt/Parlamento/Paginas/Separacao-Estado-Igrejas.aspx, last accessed on 5 May 2020.

13 Torres Gutiérrez, *El derecho*, p. 120.

14 Machado, *Liberdade Religiosa*, p. 118.

15 Machado, *Liberdade Religiosa*, p. 118.

16 Machado, *Liberdade Religiosa*, p. 119.

fail to colour some of them in red. The state may object to the appointment of Bishops, Residential Archbishops and Bishops, their assistants *cum iure successionis* and auxiliaries, parish priests, rectors of seminaries, and generally the directors and superiors of institutes or associations with legal personality having jurisdiction in one or more provinces of the country had to be Portuguese nationals. This way, the Catholic Church was kept at arm's length. Still, the Concordat was nonetheless seen by minority religious confessions as a Magna Carta of discriminatory measures towards them and privileges for the Catholic Church.[17]

All in all, this was the perfect cover for the attacks on religious freedom that followed with successive alterations to the Constitution. The neutrality of the state was compromised by the approval of provisions such as the differentiation of the regime that regulated the Catholic Church and the other religions. Those who could freely regulate themselves were now the subject of a new regulation defined by law.[18]

The Carnations Revolution of April 1974 represented a paradigm shift in the relationship between the Portuguese state and the various religious communities. Although the relationship between the Catholic Church and the New State was not absolutely linear and free from complexities, the truth is that for many revolutionaries the Catholic Church had been a cornerstone of the old political order. For this reason, the rejection of the Estado Novo would imply, sooner or later, a structural change in the relationship between religious confessions and the state, within the framework of a free and democratic constitutional order, capable of guaranteeing equal dignity and freedom to all citizens, regardless of their beliefs. religious or non-religious, and structuring an open and pluralistic public sphere, shared by different religious confessions and other ideologically motivated entities, in a climate of political contest and spiritual competition. In this context, despite its undeniable historical, social and cultural relevance in shaping the collective identity and spirit of the Portuguese people, both Catholic and non-Catholic, the Catholic Church would be treated as only one of several religious denominations.

This does not mean, however, that the change in the legal regime was abrupt. The revolutionaries did not want to throw everything away and did not intend to harass the Catholic Church in a way that might turn out to be counterproductive. On the other hand, the more conservative sectors of the democratic

---

17 Carvalho, Rita Maria Cristovam Cipriano Almeida, A Concordata de Salazar Portugal-Santa Sé 1940, (Lisboa: FCSH, UNL, 2009) pp. 7 and ff.

18 Torres Gutiérrez. El derecho, pp. 150–151.

forces recognised in the Catholic Church an important ally against the leftist Marxist sectors of the revolutionary movement. Likewise, even within the centre-left party sector there were some Catholics strongly influenced by the Church's social doctrine and its ideals of social justice and care for the most disadvantaged. It was, therefore, necessary to wait a few more years to see major adjustments in the legal regime of relations between religious confessions and the state.

The current text of the Portuguese Constitution dated 1976 includes religious freedom in Article 41. The legal text deals with the individual right in articles 1 to 3 and the institutional right in articles 4 and 5.

> Artigo 41.º—Liberdade de Consciência, de Religião e de Culto[19]
> 1. A liberdade de consciência, de religião e de culto é inviolável.
> 2. Ninguém pode ser perseguido, privado de direitos ou isento de obrigações ou deveres cívicos por causa das suas convicções ou prática religiosa.
> 3. Ninguém pode ser perguntado por qualquer autoridade acerca das suas convicções ou prática religiosa, salvo para recolha de dados estatísticos não individualmente identificáveis, nem ser prejudicado por se recusar a responder.
> 4. As igrejas e outras comunidades religiosas estão separadas do Estado e são livres na sua organização e no exercício das suas funções e do culto.
> 5. É garantida a liberdade de ensino de qualquer religião praticado no âmbito da respetiva confissão, bem como a utilização de meios de comunicação social próprios para o prosseguimento das suas atividades.
> 6. É garantido o direito à objeção de consciência, nos termos da lei.

The title of the Article refers to the provision of three distinct rights: freedom of conscience, religion and worship.

First, the right to freedom of conscience, religion and worship is inviolable. In whatever situation, this right cannot be limited, hindered or suppressed in any form. The Constitution thus recognises the close relationship between the dignity of the human person and individual freedom in matters related to the search for the truth about the ultimate and transcendent reality of things and the origin, meaning and destiny of human existence. Public authorities have no jurisdiction in these matters, nor can they claim to dictate and impose on the people particular guidance on them. It is for each individual to take a position

19 https://dre.pt/web/guest/legislacao-consolidada/-/lc/337/202005051037/128000/diploma/indice?q=constitui%C3%A7%C3%A3o+da+rep%C3%BAblica, last accessed on 5 May 2020.

on these issues. Individual religious freedom, therefore, constitutes an important limitation on the sovereign power of the state. Freedom of conscience, religion and worship is thus a powerful antidote to any authoritarian or totalitarian claims of political power. At the same time, these freedoms constitute a structuring, guiding and positively conforming principle when it comes to the exercise of that same power.

Freedom of Religion, as conceived in the Portuguese Constitution, introduces three dimensions concerning the duties and obligations of the state in this matter. The state cannot hinder someone in or require them to adhere to a certain belief. Furthermore, the state must allow and provide conditions for those who wish to comply with duties that may arise from their belief or religion. Added to this, the state cannot require or guarantee through the law the fulfilment of those obligations. If there are conditions that restrict or impose the practice of a determined religion, there is no freedom of religion.[20] It is recognised that when public authorities seek to control and determine convictions about the most intimate, personal and existential feelings of individuals, they undermine the essential core of their human dignity, denying its uniqueness and seeking to destroy it and subordinate it to the state.

The legal text goes on to determine that no one can be persecuted, deprived of rights or exempted from civic obligations or duties on the ground of their convictions or religious observance (Article 41 (2)),[21] no-one can be asked by any authority to declare their religion, except for statistical purposes—where the information should be anonymised—and be affected in any way by refusing to answer. (Article 41(3)). This is how the concrete "no-interference" obligation of the state is translated into practice.

If freedom of conscience is inherently an individual right, freedom of religion, on the other hand, includes both individual and collective dimensions. This collective dimension is expressed in Article 41 (4) of the Constitution. In addition to removing barriers to religious freedom and protecting the free exercise of religion by individuals and religious communities, the state should seek to contribute to the creation of the necessary and appropriate normative, institutional, regulatory and factual conditions enabling effective exercise of the freedom of conscience and religion, in the most diverse ways and the most diverse contexts.

---

20 Miranda, Jorge, Medeiros, Rui, *Constituição Portuguesa Anotada, Volume I*, (Coimbra: Coimbra Editora, 2010), p. 909.

21 Canotilho, J.J. Gomes, Moreira, Vital, *Constituição da República Portuguesa: anotada, Volume I* (Coimbra: Coimbra Editora, 2014), p. 609.

1.1.1 *Organisation of Religious Communities*

In principle in this collective dimension the Constitution clarifies the separation between churches and religious communities and the state and underlines their freedom to organise and operate freely in their functions and worship.[22] This is of great importance. This provision gives constitutional relevance, status, dignity and visibility to minority religious confessions, whether Christian (e.g. Orthodox, Protestant and Evangelical)[23] or non-Christian (e.g. Islamic, Jewish, Buddhist or Hindu). They could all now claim the dignity of their recognition as equals before the Constitution and the law. They could from now on consider freely developing their own religious activities without being impeded or disturbed, in law or fact, by a dominant theological-political coalition.

This independence of the churches and religious communities from the state does not limit the possibility of there being differentiated regulations between them. When the constitutional text was drafted, the 1940s Concordat with the Catholic Church was in place and there was no wish in the Constitutional Assembly that it should be discontinued.[24] There is, therefore, the ability to create specific regulations and agreements between the state and specific religious communities, as happened with the agreement with the Ismaili Imamat which we will analyse further.[25]

1.1.2 *Religious Autonomy of Teaching and Expression*

Finally, the Constitution guarantees the freedom to teach any religion within the ambit of the religious belief in question. This right allows teaching inside and outside places of worship. The training of clerics is included in this freedom. Article 75 (2) of the Constitution establishes that the state should recognise and inspect private and cooperative education; however religious education may not be inspected by the state.[26]

Different religious belief systems express a particular view of the world. The same is true of non-religious belief systems. There is no point of absolute neutrality from which to judge which of the different worldviews is true. Nor can

22 Torres Gutiérrez, *El derecho*, pp. 216–217.

23 In Portugal, it is common to distinguish between Protestants derived from the Reformation (eg Lutherans, Calvinists, Presbyterians, Methodists, Baptists) and the more recent evangelicals, with special emphasis on neo-Pentecostals and defenders of the prosperity gospel, although some Christian denominations could fall into both categories.

24 Machado, Jónatas, *O Regime Concordatário entre a "Libertas Ecclesiae" e a Liberdade Religiosa—Liberdade de Religião ou liberdade da Igreja?* (Coimbra: Coimbra Editora, 1993), p. 75.

25 See below—2.1. Agreement between Portugal and the Shia Imami Imamat Ismaili.

26 Canotilho, Moreira, Constituição da República, p. 615.

constitutional law claim absolute worldview neutrality for itself. Most of the presuppositions, values and principles of modern constitutional law are the distilled product of the elaboration and theoretical discussion persistently and patiently carried out over many centuries in European convents, monasteries, churches, universities, castles and palaces, building on the philosophical and religious roots of Western civilisation. It is therefore important that religious confessions can freely teach their doctrines and subject them to argumentative testing and critical control in the public discourse of the democratic constitutional order.

Article 41 (5) of the Constitution also establishes that the state must guarantee the freedom to use the religion's own media for the pursuit of its activities. This means that religious communities can own private media channels, and access radio and television broadcasting by licence like any other private entity. All the churches and religious communities also have the right to broadcasting time on the public radio and television service, as the Constitution considers religious communities to be social organisations of national scope (Article 40 (1) of the Constitution).[27] Religious freedom implies the freedom to communicate religious ideas in the context of a polycentric communication structure where a wide range of communicative opportunities is guaranteed. These rights, in their collective dimension, are set out in detail in the Religious Freedom Act.

The Constitution is clear on freedom of religion as an inviolable right, and the ordinary law goes deeper into every dimension of this right. Religious communities benefit from a vast freedom to practise and to exist within their community. This is very important. Religion is concerned with the most diverse aspects of individual and collective life. It is therefore natural and healthy for religious confessions to participate in the discussion of issues of interest to all individuals and the entire political community. All confessions are an integral part of the public sphere. Their members are full citizens, members of the political community, and pay their taxes to the state budget. As a result, all religious denominations, large or small, rich or poor, not only can mobilise their own resources to pursue activities that they feel are appropriate to the fulfilment of their religious goals, but in some cases also have the support of public resources, which belong equally to all citizens, for this purpose.

27 Canotilho, Moreira, *Constituição da República*, pp. 615–616.

1.2 Legal Recognition of Churches and Religious Communities

A very important development in this area was the passing in Portugal of the Religious Freedom Act, Act no. 16/2001. The promoter of the initiative was Dr Vera Jardim, who was then Minister of Justice, and the role of Councillor José de Sousa Brito, Judge of the Constitutional Court, in the material preparation of the legislative proposal should be highlighted.

In this initiative one can feel the influence of two relevant sectors of the socialist party, namely the secular Republican on the one hand and the progressive Catholic on the other. The Socialist Party played an important role in extending religious freedom and deepening the principle of the separation of religious confessions from the state, without ever falling into those forms of secularist and anti-religious radicalism, or specifically anti-Christianity, which are seen in some other countries. Even in discussing more fractious issues (e.g. abortion, same-sex marriage, euthanasia), the Socialist Party has never harassed the Catholic Church and never understood the secularisation of the state as prohibiting any form of public cooperation with it or with the other religious communities.

For its part, the Catholic Church has in some cases been an important ally of the Socialist Party, particularly when it comes to social policies of income redistribution and the correction of social inequalities, even though there are still moral issues of clear and deep disagreement. It is in this context that the law of religious liberty and subsequent developments must be understood.

Act no. 16/2001 regulates freedom of religion by putting into practice the rights set out in the Constitution. The legal recognition of churches and religious communities in Portugal is the subject of one of its Chapters. Chapter v defines the statutes of churches and religious communities. In the Portuguese legal system we can find different levels of the status of religious corporate bodies. In this qualification we can observe a disparity in the rights and guarantees given, noting that the basic form of entity has access to all the constitutional rights and guarantees.[28]

---

28 Argiolas, Davide, A Responsabilidade Civil das Entidades Religiosas (Lisbon: Petrony Editora, 2017), p. 212.

1.3 Religious Entities with No Juridical Personality

Everybody has the right to gather and associate with others for religious ends. This is the essence of article 8(f) of the Religious Freedom Act.

> Artigo 8.º—Conteúdo da liberdade de consciência, de religião e de culto[29]
> A liberdade de consciência, religião e de culto compreende o direito de:
> (…)
> f) Reunir-se, manifestar-se e associar-se com outros de acordo com as próprias convicções em matéria religiosa, sem outros limites além dos previstos no artigo 45.º e 46.º da Constituição;
> (…)

This provision allows religious entities to exist without being registered. However, they are restricted in their exercise of other rights which derive from religious freedom, such as the freedom formally to organise their churches and religious communities (article 22), the freedom to perform religious activities and worship (article 23),[30] the freedom to perform non-religious activities, such as founding schools and doing charitable work (article 27), the right to use for religious purposes property intended for other purposes (article 29) and the protection of religious assets (article 30). All these rights require the existence of legal personality to be exercised.[31]

Paragraph (f) also refers to the limitations imposed by Articles 45 and 46 of the Portuguese Constitution. They set out the limits of the right to meet and to demonstrate and the right to freedom of association.

The Portuguese legal system allows everyone to express their confession, religion or belief without official registration, as long as the limitations on the rights to meet and demonstrate and to associate are respected.

This is a basic and minimal level of organisation, based above all on the exercise of freedom of religion and assembly. In essence, it is suitable for those people who enjoy the experience of spirituality but distrust organised religion. It is, therefore, an option that is open to those who are most comfortable with this informal type of religious experience. It is also suitable for the early and embryonic manifestations of religious experience.

29 https://dre.pt/web/guest/legislacao-consolidada/-/lc/106639383/202005051052/73413222/diploma/indice?q=lei+da+liberdade+religiosa, last accessed on 5 May 2020.

30 As we will see below, this right allows religious communities to, for example, assist their members in religious matters or to appoint and train their ministers.

31 Torres Gutiérrez, *El Derecho*, p. 289.

At a slightly higher level, it is possible for several individuals to create a private-law association for religious purposes, even if they do not want to give it the designation and status of religious confession. For this purpose they may use the Civil Code, which establishes the typical structure of such an association, which must have a board, a general assembly and a committee of auditors. The associative form is compatible with the pursuit of various purposes, including those of a religious nature. In practice, many non-Catholic religious confessions have resorted to this associative form. For all intents and purposes, they constituted private-law associations like any other.

1.4 Registered Religious Communities

The Chapter on the statute of churches and religious communities starts by defining which entities can acquire legal personality as religious corporate bodies. Besides obtaining legal personality, registered religious communities are entitled to a broader spectrum of collective rights. This form of registration does not require the formalities required of private associations or foundations in public law, i.e. legal personality is acquired without any juridical formality.[32]

> Artigo 33.º—Personalidade jurídica das pessoas coletivas religiosas[33]
> Podem adquirir personalidade jurídica pela inscrição no registo das pessoas coletivas religiosas, que é criado no departamento governamental competente:
> a) As igrejas e demais comunidades religiosas de âmbito nacional ou, em sua vez, as organizações representativas dos crentes residentes em território nacional;
> b) As igrejas e demais comunidades religiosas de âmbito regional ou local;
> c) Os institutos de vida consagrada e outros institutos, com a natureza de associações ou de fundações, fundados ou reconhecidos pelas pessoas coletivas referidas nas alíneas a) e b) para a prossecução dos seus fins religiosos;
> d) As federações ou as associações de pessoas coletivas referidas nas alíneas anteriores.

32 Argiolas, *A Responsabilidade*, p. 214.

33 https://dre.pt/web/guest/legislacao-consolidada/-/lc/106639383/202005051252/73413249/diploma/indice, last accessed on 5 May 2020.

Four different entities can apply for this form of registration: churches and other religious communities of national scope or their representative organisations of believers residing in the Portuguese territory; churches and other religious communities of regional and local scope; religious orders and other institutions with the character of associations or foundations, established or recognised by the corporate religious bodies mentioned; and foundations or associations of the corporate religious bodies mentioned.

> Artigo 34.º—Requisitos da inscrição no registo[34]
> O pedido de inscrição é dirigido ao departamento governamental competente e instruído com os estatutos e outros documentos que permitam inscrever:
> a) O nome, que deverá permitir distingui-lo de qualquer outra pessoa coletiva religiosa existente em Portugal;
> b) A constituição, instituição ou estabelecimento em Portugal da organização correspondente à igreja ou comunidade religiosa ou o ato de constituição ou fundação e, eventualmente, também o de reconhecimento da pessoa coletiva religiosa;
> c) A sede em Portugal;
> d) Os fins religiosos;
> e) Os bens ou serviços que integram ou deverão integrar o património;
> f) As disposições sobre formação, composição, competência e funcionamento dos seus órgãos;
> g) As disposições sobre a extinção da pessoa colectiva;
> h) O modo de designação e os poderes dos seus representantes;
> i) A identificação dos titulares dos órgãos em efectividade de funções e dos representantes e especificação da competência destes últimos.

The article goes on to set out what information should be provided when an entity applies for the status: its name (which should be distinct from those of other religious corporate bodies that already exist in Portugal) (point a); the address of its registered head office in Portugal (point c); its religious purposes (point d); a list of the goods or services that comprise the estate (point e); the rules governing the formation, composition, competence and operation of their bodies (point f); rules for the dissolution of the corporate body (point g); the method of appointment of their representatives and the powers of those

34 https://dre.pt/web/guest/legislacao-consolidada/-/lc/106639383/202005051352/73413250/diploma/indice, last accessed on 5 May 2020.

representatives (point h); and identification of the effective leaders, their representatives and their competences (point i).

Point b) also requires the constitution, institution or establishment in Portugal of the organisation corresponding to the church or religious community or the deed of the constitution of the association or establishment and the recognition of the religious corporate body to be presented for inspection. When there is no recognition of churches or religious communities previously established, article 35 adds two complementary requirements.

> Artigo 35.º—Inscrição das igrejas e comunidades religiosas[35]
> A inscrição das igrejas ou comunidades religiosas de âmbito nacional, ou de âmbito regional ou local, quando não sejam criadas ou reconhecidas pelas anteriores, é ainda instruída com prova documental:
> a) Dos princípios gerais da doutrina e da descrição geral de prática religiosa e dos atos do culto e, em especial, dos direitos e deveres dos crentes relativamente à igreja ou comunidade religiosa, devendo ser ainda apresentado um sumário de todos estes elementos;
> b) Da sua existência em Portugal, com especial incidência sobre os factos que atestam a presença social organizada, a prática religiosa e a duração em Portugal.

Applicants should also present documentary evidence of the general principles of the doctrine and a description of the religious practices and acts of worship undertaken, particularly the rights and duties of members in relation to the church or religious community and how long the religious practice has existed in Portugal, particularly evidence of a socially organised presence in the country.

The same conditions that are set out in articles 33 to 35 are applied to the registration of representative organisations of believers by churches and religious communities with a supranational scope in article 36.

> Artigo 36.º—Inscrição de organização representativa de crentes residentes em território nacional[36]
> 1—As igrejas e comunidades religiosas que tenham âmbito supranacional podem instituir uma organização representativa dos crentes residentes no território nacional, que requererá a sua própria inscrição no registo,

35 https://dre.pt/web/guest/legislacao-consolidada/-/lc/106639383/202005051452/73413251/diploma/indice, last accessed on 5 May 2020.

36 https://dre.pt/web/guest/legislacao-consolidada/-/lc/106639383/202005051552/73413252/diploma/indice

em vez da inscrição da parte da igreja ou comunidade religiosa existente no território nacional.
2—A inscrição está sujeita às mesmas condições da inscrição de igrejas ou comunidades religiosas de âmbito nacional.

When the requirements of the abovementioned articles have been fulfilled the church or religious community is entered in the National Registry of Religious Entities (NRRE) which is regulated by Executive Legislative Decree (ELD)[37] no. 134/2003, of 28 of June.[38] The ability quickly and easily to acquire legal personality through the national registration system of religious legal persons is an important guarantee of collective religious freedom. Entry in the NRRE guarantees the ability to exercise almost all the institutional rights of religious freedom, giving religious confessions the ability freely to develop their activities in the most diverse areas. Recently, several news outlets—drawing on data collected by the Minister of Justice and the Commission on Religious Freedom—have reported that between 2006 and 2018 860 religious entities were created. That means that around five religious entities were created every month. About 85 per cent of the communities that register are Evangelical, but the number of Orthodox and Protestant communities has also been increasing. Islamic, Hindu and Buddhist communities are also increasing, albeit to a lesser extent. There are no hard data on the number of believers who belong to the new religious communities.[39] The explanation may be due, on the one hand, to the arrival of immigrants from Brazil, Africa and Eastern European countries who profess other religions, and also to the fact that the churches want to enjoy the tax benefits available. These include, among others, exemption from corporate income tax, municipal property tax and gift and inheritance tax. This facility demon-

37 In the Portuguese Legal System the Government, as the holder of the state's executive power, also has legislative power with regard to subjects that are not exclusively within the competence of the Parliament. It can also legislate on fundamental rights issues whenever so authorised by the Parliament. Executive Legislative Decrees are numbered in order of publication in the official journal and together with the year in which they are published. Further information on Articles 164 and 165 of the Portuguese Constitution is available at https://dre.pt/web/guest/legislacao-consolidada/-/lc/34520775/view, last accessed on 5 May 2020.

38 EDL no. 134/2003 which regulates the National Registry for Religious Entities is available at https://dre.pt/web/guest/pesquisa/-/search/693255/details/normal?q=decreto-lei+134%2F2003, last accessed on 5 May 2020.

39 "Nos últimos 12 anos, foram legalmente criadas 860 novas igrejas em Portugal" [In the last 12 years, 860 new churches were legally created in Portugal], *Observador*, 01.12.2019, https://observador.pt/2019/12/01/nos-ultimos-12-anos-foram-legalmente-criadas-860-novas-igrejas-em-portugal/, last accessed on 5 May 2020.

strates how easy it is to exercise collective religious freedom through a system that, in the area of religious freedom, significantly reduces transaction costs.

After 30 years of organised presence in the country, churches and religious communities can apply for a settlement certification (*Radicação*).

Artigo 37.º—Igrejas e comunidades religiosas radicadas no País[40]
1—Consideram-se radicadas no País as igrejas e comunidades religiosas inscritas com garantia de duração, sendo a qualificação atestada pelo membro do Governo competente em razão da matéria, em vista do número de crentes e da história da sua existência em Portugal, depois de ouvir a Comissão da Liberdade Religiosa.
2—O atestado não poderá ser requerido antes de 30 anos de presença social organizada no País, salvo se se tratar de igreja ou comunidade religiosa fundada no estrangeiro há mais de 60 anos. O atestado é averbado no registo.
3—O requerimento do atestado será instruído com a prova dos factos que o fundamentam, aplicando-se o disposto no artigo 38.º

The settlement request is reviewed by the Commission on Religious Freedom[41] and witnessed by the Minister of Justice. Churches or religious communities must have had a presence in Portugal for 30 years or more, or abroad for 60 years or more. Only entities that are registered in the National Registry for Religious Entities can apply for this status.[42]

The law automatically entitles registered religious communities to several rights that religious communities registered as associations[43] or non-registered religious communities cannot benefit from.[44]

Ministers of religion have the right to benefit from the general social security system, under the terms determined by law, if their religious community is registered as such and their religious activity is their principal activity (Article 16, 4). They also benefit from the professional privilege of confidentiality (Article 16, 2) regarding their relationship with members of their religious confession or with individuals to whom they give spiritual counselling. This is a

40 https://dre.pt/web/guest/legislacao-consolidada/-/lc/106639383/202005051652/73413253/diploma/indice, last accessed on 5 May 2020.

41 The Commission on Religious Freedom was created by the Religious Freedom Act and its functions, competences, composition and operation are regulated in Chapter VI of the Act.

42 Argiolas, A Responsabilidade, p. 214.

43 See below—1.5 Religious Communities as Associations.

44 Torres Gutiérrez, *El derecho*, p. 293.

right that, in addition to cementing trust in the relationship between individuals and the minister of religion, contributes to the trust and credibility of the institution itself, assuming both an individual and a collective dimension.

When there are military obligations to be fulfilled by students who are being trained to be ministers of religion, their obligations are fulfilled in chaplaincy functions,[45] health services and social activities, unless they want to provide armed service. The law also allows excuse from classification and selection for military service and postponement of military service if the person in question is attending a training course for ministers of religion (Article 17). Ministers of religion or religious who live a consecrated life can be exempt from jury service (Article 18).[46]

Registered religious communities also have the right to ask the Minister of Education to be allowed to provide religious education in primary and secondary public schools (Article 24,1).[47]

The right of registered religious communities to use public broadcasting channels to disseminate their beliefs is defined in Article 25. There is also a broad catalogue of tax incentives that registered religious communities can benefit from, which cannot be claimed by other religious communities that do not have this status.

Religious communities that are certified as settled in Portugal are entitled to more rights, such as the recognition of religiously celebrated marriages with civil effects (Article 19);[48] the right to be represented in the Commission for the Religious Persuasions' Broadcasting Time which decides on the distribution of broadcasting time amongst registered religious communities (Article 25, 3);[49] the right to take part in the Commission on Religious Freedom (Article 56);[50] and eligibility to receive 0.5 per cent of the income tax of registered members (Article 32, 4).[51/52]

It is also relevant to mention that settled religious communities can develop special cooperation agreements with the State, which must be approved by law (Article 49).[53]

---

45 See below—9. Islamic Chaplaincy in Public Institutions.
46 Torres Gutiérrez, *El derecho*, p. 292.
47 Torres Gutiérrez, *El derecho*, pp. 292–293. See below—7.2 Religious Education.
48 See below—15.2. Marriage and Divorce.
49 See below—3.4 Commission for the Religious Persuasions' Broadcasting Time.
50 See below—3.3. Commission on Religious Freedom.
51 See below—3.2. Tax benefits.
52 Torres Gutiérrez, *El derecho*, pp. 294–295.
53 Torres Gutiérrez, *El derecho*, p. 295.

The Islamic Community of Lisbon is a settled religious community in Portugal and takes part in the Commission on Religious Freedom and the Commission for the Religious Persuasions' Broadcasting Time.

1.5 Religious Communities as Associations

These entities have legal personality equivalent to that of a private law association. Before the Religious Freedom Act was passed these entities would register with the Ministry of Justice in a special registry. With the new Act in 2001 the registry was abolished and the entries in it were transferred into the National Registry of Collective Entities, the general registry for private corporate bodies.

Today, article 44 of the Religious Freedom Act regulates those private corporate bodies with religious objectives that can acquire legal personality with certain privileges through compliance with the rules established in the Civil Code.[54]

> Artigo 44.º—Pessoas coletivas privadas com fins religiosos[55]
> As associações e fundações com fins religiosos podem ainda adquirir personalidade jurídica nos termos previstos no Código Civil para as pessoas coletivas privadas, ficando então sujeitas às respetivas normas, exceto quanto à sua atividade com fins religiosos.

Article 44 provides special treatment for religious entities that register as private-law associations and foundations. These are subject to the Civil Code rules that regulate private corporate bodies in every aspect of their activity, except as far as their religious objectives are concerned. These entities must prove their religious status if they wish to use the effects of this regime against third parties and can appeal to the appropriate courts to do so.[56]

This solution was introduced by Act no. 16/2001, which replaced the former Religious Freedom Act of 1971. The transitional regime for these entities is set out in article 63.

---

54 The Civil Code was enacted in 1966 and has been altered and updated ever since.

55 https://dre.pt/web/guest/legislacao-consolidada/-/lc/106639383/202005052352/73413260/diploma/indice, last accessed on 5 May 2020.

56 Argiolas, A Responsabilidade, p. 213.

Artigo 63.º—Confissões religiosas e associações religiosas não católicas atualmente inscritas[57]
1—As confissões religiosas e as associações religiosas não católicas inscritas no correspondente registo do departamento governamental competente conservam a sua personalidade jurídica e a sua capacidade, passando a estar sujeitas à presente lei quanto às suas atividades religiosas, nos termos do artigo 44.º
2—As mesmas confissões e associações podem requerer a sua conversão em uma pessoa coletiva religiosa, nos termos dos artigos 34.º a 40.º, mediante o preenchimento dos respetivos requisitos, no prazo de três anos desde a entrada em vigor da presente lei.
3—Se o não fizerem, passarão a estar inscritas apenas no Registo Nacional das Pessoas Coletivas, para onde serão remetidos os processos e os documentos que serviram de base aos respetivos registos.
4—Passado o prazo referido no n.º 2, é extinto o atual registo de confissões religiosas e associações religiosas não católicas do Ministério da Justiça.

The transitional provisions allowed religious denominations and non-Catholic religious associations that were registered with the Ministry of Justice to maintain their legal status, including them in the new framework provided by article 44. For a period of three years, these denominations and associations could ask to be converted into religious corporate bodies, under the regime set out in articles 34 to 40 of the Religious Freedom Act (number 2 above).[58]

After the three year deadline, the registry of religious denominations and non-Catholic religious associations was closed (point 4); and the associations that chose not to ask to be converted into religious corporate bodies retained their legal personality and are now registered in the National Registry for Corporate Bodies (RNPC) (point 3).

57 https://dre.pt/web/guest/legislacao-consolidada/-/lc/106639383/202005060152/73413283/diploma/indice, last accessed on 5 May 2020.

58 See above—1.4 Registered Religious Communities.

1.6 Recognition of Ministers of Religion

The recognition of ministers of religion is referred to in Article 15.

Artigo 15.º—Ministros do culto[59]
1—Ministros do culto são as pessoas como tais consideradas segundo as normas da respetiva igreja ou comunidade religiosa.
2—A qualidade de ministro de culto é certificada pelos órgãos competentes da respetiva igreja ou comunidade religiosa, que igualmente credenciam os respetivos ministros para a prática de atos determinados.
3—A autenticação dos certificados e das credenciais referidos no número anterior compete ao registo das pessoas coletivas religiosas.

The law considers ministers of religion to be people who are recognised as such by the regulations of their churches or religious communities (Article 15 (1)).[60] The status of minister of religion is certified by the competent bodies of the respective churches or religious communities, which are also allowed to certify ministers for different and specific acts (Article 15 (2)). Credentials and certifications are authenticated by the registration offices of religious corporate bodies (Article 15 (3)).

The defining of the formal criteria regarding what constitutes a minister of religion has been transferred from the state to the churches or religious communities. In this way, the state protects the freedom and autonomy given to these entities, introducing in numbers 2 and 3 instruments that can prevent abuses and maintain a balance in this formal criterion defined by churches and religious communities.[61]

Once certified, ministers of religion are entitled to several rights, set out in article 16.

Artigo 16.º—Direitos dos ministros de culto[62]
1—Os ministros do culto têm a liberdade de exercer o seu ministério.
2—Os ministros do culto não podem ser perguntados pelos magistrados ou outras autoridades sobre factos e coisas de que tenham tido conhecimento por motivo do seu ministério.

---

59 https://dre.pt/web/guest/legislacao-consolidada/-/lc/106639383/202005060352/73413229/diploma/indice, last accessed on 5 May 2020.

60 Torres Gutiérrez, *El derecho*, p. 299.

61 Argiolas, *A responsabilidade*, p. 245.

62 https://dre.pt/web/guest/legislacao-consolidada/-/lc/106639383/202005060452/73413230/diploma/indice, last accessed on 5 May 2020.

3—O exercício do ministério é considerado atividade profissional do ministro do culto quando lhe proporciona meios de sustento, bastando como prova destes para efeito da autorização de residência a ministros do culto estrangeiros a sua garantia pela respetiva igreja ou comunidade religiosa.
4—Os ministros do culto das igrejas e demais comunidades religiosas inscritas têm direito às prestações do sistema de segurança social nos termos da lei, sendo obrigatoriamente inscritos pela igreja ou comunidade religiosa a que pertençam, salvo se exercerem por forma secundária a atividade religiosa e o exercício da atividade principal não religiosa determinar a inscrição obrigatória num regime de segurança social.
5—Para os efeitos dos dois números anteriores, equiparam-se aos ministros do culto os membros de institutos de vida consagrada e outras pessoas que exercem profissionalmente atividades religiosas e que, como tais, sejam certificadas pela igreja ou comunidade religiosa a que pertençam.

Ministers of religion have, first, the freedom to carry out their ministry. They are also entitled to professional confidentiality—number 2 states that magistrates and other authorities cannot ask them about facts and matters that have come to their knowledge through the exercise of their ministry.

The law also provides that ministers of religion have the right to have their ministry considered as their professional activity when it is their means of support (article 16 (3)). As referred to above,[63] they also have the right to access the general social security system, as long as their church or religious community is a registered religious community under Portuguese law (article 16 (4)).[64]

In article 16 (5), the rights of ministers of religion also apply to members of consecrated institutions who practise their religious activities professionally and are, therefore, certified by their church or religious communities to do so.

Ministers of religion also have the right to fulfil their military obligations by giving religious assistance, or carrying out health or social activities (article 17 (1)) and are exempt from jury service (article 18).[65]

63 See above—1.4. Registered Religious Communities.

64 Argiolas, *A responsabilidade*, p. 243.

65 Argiolas, *A responsabilidade*, pp. 243–244.

CHAPTER 2

Relations between the State and Islam

The relationship between the state and Churches and religious communities is regulated by Chapter v of the Religious Freedom Act. There is no specific legislation that regulates a special relationship between the state and Islam, so we apply the general legislation applicable to relations between churches and religious communities and the state.

In Chapter v of the Act we find the process that regulates possible agreements:

> Artigo 45.º—Acordos entre igrejas ou comunidades religiosas e o Estado[1]
> As igrejas ou comunidades religiosas radicadas no País ou as federações em que as mesmas se integram podem propor a celebração de acordos com o Estado sobre matérias de interesse comum.

This ability to propose agreements to the state is provided only for Churches or religious communities or federations that are settled in Portugal.

> Artigo 46.º—Processo de celebração dos acordos[2]
> 1—A proposta de acordo é apresentada em requerimento de abertura de negociações dirigido ao membro do Governo responsável pela área da justiça, acompanhado de documentação comprovativa da verificação da conformidade referida na alínea a) do artigo 47.º
> 2—Depois de ouvir sobre a proposta de acordo a Comissão da Liberdade Religiosa, o membro do Governo responsável pela área da justiça pode:
> a) Recusar justificadamente a negociação do acordo;
> b) Nomear uma comissão negociadora, composta por representantes dos ministérios interessados e por igual número de cidadãos portugueses designados pela igreja ou comunidade religiosa, com o encargo de elaborar um projeto de acordo ou um relato das razões da sua impraticabilidade. O presidente da Comissão é designado pelo Ministro.

1 https://dre.pt/web/guest/legislacao-consolidada/-/lc/106639383/202005060652/73413262/diploma/indice, last accessed on 5 May 2020.

2 https://dre.pt/web/guest/legislacao-consolidada/-/lc/106639383/202005060752/73413263/diploma/indice, last accessed on 5 May 2020.

The process leading to an agreement starts with an application requesting the opening of negotiations and addressed to the Minister of Justice (or to whoever is responsible for the Justice area).[3] After hearing the Commission on Religious Freedom about the possibility of an agreement, the Ministry of Justice decides between justifiably refusing the agreement or, upon a positive analysis and outcome, appointing a negotiating committee. The negotiating committee is composed of representatives of the Ministries relevant to the subject of the agreement (e.g. if the agreement concerns education, the Ministry of Education should be involved in the negotiations) and an equal number of Portuguese citizens nominated by the church or religious community. The committee is responsible for developing a draft agreement or a report on the reasons why the agreement cannot be made. The Chairman of the Committee is appointed by the Minister.

> Artigo 47.º—Fundamentos de recusa da negociação do acordo[4]
> São fundamentos de recusa da negociação do acordo:
> a) Não estar assegurado que as normas internas ou a prática religiosa da igreja ou comunidade religiosa se conformem com as normas da ordem jurídica portuguesa;
> b) Não terem decorrido cinco anos sobre a recusa de proposta anterior;
> c) Não ser necessária a aprovação de uma nova lei para alcançar os objetivos práticos da proposta;
> d) Não merecer aprovação o conteúdo essencial da proposta.

The Act also lists the acceptable reasons for refusing to negotiate an agreement. There are grounds for refusing to negotiate an agreement when the church or religious community cannot ensure compliance with the Portuguese legal system within its internal regulations or religious practice (paragraph a). Article 47 also provides for situations where there is no need to approve a new law to meet the requirements of the proposed agreement (paragraph c) or when the essential content of the proposal does not need approval within the framework

---

3 According to article 8 (3) of the EDL no. 123/2011 it is in the competence of the Ministry of Justice to give support to the Commission on Religious Freedom "3—A SG assegura o apoio administrativo e logístico à Comissão da Liberdade Religiosa, órgão independente de consulta da Assembleia da República e do Governo, objeto de regulamentação em diploma próprio.", in https://dre.pt/web/guest/legislacao-consolidada/-/lc/107981220/202001071731/exportPdf/normal/1/cacheLevelPage?_LegislacaoConsolidada_WAR_drefrontofficeportlet_rp=indice, last accessed on 5 May 2020.

4 https://dre.pt/web/guest/legislacao-consolidada/-/lc/106639383/202005060852/73413264/diploma/indice, last accessed on 5 May 2020.

determined by the law (paragraph d). When an agreement is refused, churches and religious communities can initiate a new negotiations for an agreement only after five years (paragraph b).

When no impediment is raised, the agreement is approved by the Council of Ministers. Then it is signed by the Prime Minister and other Ministers who are competent as regards the subjects agreed upon and the representative of the church, religious community or federation (article 48 (1)).

Artigo 48.º—Celebração do acordo[5]
1—Uma vez aprovado em Conselho de Ministros, o acordo é assinado pelo Primeiro-Ministro e pelos ministros competentes em razão da matéria, do lado do Governo, e pelos representantes da igreja ou da comunidade religiosa ou da federação.
2—O acordo só entrará em vigor depois da sua aprovação por lei da Assembleia da República.

The agreement enters into force after the bill is passed in Parliament (article 48 (2)). The bill approving the agreement is sent to the Assembly of the Republic to be voted on and approved (article 49).

Artigo 49.º—Proposta de lei de aprovação do acordo[6]
O acordo é apresentado à Assembleia da República com a proposta da lei que o aprova.

Article 50 permits the agreement to be altered at any time before it is approved in the Assembly of the Republic. These amendments should be agreed by both parties and the Assembly of the Republic informed accordingly.

Artigo 50.º—Alterações do acordo[7]
Até à deliberação da Assembleia da República que aprovar o acordo, este pode ser alterado por acordo das partes, devendo qualquer alteração ser imediatamente comunicada à Assembleia da República.

5 https://dre.pt/web/guest/legislacao-consolidada/-/lc/106639383/202005060952/73413265/diploma/indice, last accessed on 5 May 2020.

6 https://dre.pt/web/guest/legislacao-consolidada/-/lc/106639383/202005061052/73413266/diploma/indice, last accessed on 5 May 2020.

7 https://dre.pt/web/guest/legislacao-consolidada/-/lc/106639383/202005061152/73413267/diploma/indice, last accessed on 5 May 2020.

The law also leaves open the possibility of agreements with the state, autonomous regions and municipalities that do not need a law of approval. This way, the law extends the ability to make agreements to other religious corporate bodies that are not settled[8] in Portugal.

> Artigo 51.º—Outros acordos[9]
> As pessoas coletivas religiosas podem celebrar outros acordos com o Estado, as Regiões Autónomas e as autarquias locais para a realização dos seus fins, que não envolvam a aprovação de uma lei.

From the analysis of this Chapter of the Religious Freedom Act we can clearly identify the duality of the Portuguese regime on churches and religious communities. The relationship between Portugal and the Holy See is regulated by the Concordat,[10] whereas the relationship between the Portuguese state and other churches and religious communities is regulated by the law and the regime we have just analysed.[11]

It is important to understand whether the principle of non-discrimination, one of the pillars of the collective right of religious freedom, is upheld. This is referred to in article 2 of the Religious Freedom Act which, as mentioned, substantiates the right to freedom of conscience, of religion and of form of worship enshrined in the Portuguese Constitution, which states that no-one can be privileged, benefitted from, aggrieved, persecuted or deprived of any right or exempted from any duty on account of his or her conditions or religious practice. Number 2 reinforces the equality by declaring that the state should not discriminate against any church or religious community in relation to others.[12]

---

8 As we have seen, article 45 determines that the regime of Chapter V—Agreements between religious corporate bodies and the State applies only to churches and religious communities that are settled in Portugal. The settlement criteria are determined in article 37 of the Religious Freedom Act.

9 https://dre.pt/web/guest/legislacao-consolidada/-/lc/106639383/202005061252/73413268/diploma/indice, last accessed on 5 May 2020.

10 The 2004 Concordat came into being as an update to the 1940s Concordat with the Holy See. It assumes a *quasi*-international treaty text and it considers different areas such as: juridical personality and autonomy of the Catholic Church, recognition of religious marriage, religious assistance, education, patrimonial regimes and economic aspects. To develop this subject further see Torres Gutiérrez, *El derecho*.

11 Canotilho, José Joaquim Gomes, Machado, Jónatas, "Metódica Multinível: Acordos Internacionais do Estado Português com Comunidades Religiosas", *Revista de Legislação e Jurisprudência*, 3963 (2010), p. 258.

12 Canotilho, Machado, "Metódica Multinível", p. 258.

Artigo 2.º—Princípio da Igualdade[13]
1—Ninguém pode ser privilegiado, beneficiado, prejudicado, perseguido, privado de qualquer direito ou isento de qualquer dever por causa das suas convicções ou prática religiosa.
2—O Estado não discriminará nenhuma igreja ou comunidade religiosa relativamente às outras.

There is a clear affirmation of and commitment of the Portuguese state to protecting the freedom of religion in its individual and collective dimensions. This paves the way to the acceptance of an agreement with a Shia Islamic Community, the Ismaili Imamat, that regulates several points of the relationship with the Portuguese state, as we will analyse next.

It is also fundamental to understand that the agreement arises from the application of Chapter V of the Religious Freedom Act. However, these agreements are not a requirement for churches and religious communities to settle in Portugal or to exercise any of the rights that the law grants them.

2.1 Agreement between Portugal and the Shia Imami Ismaili Muslims

The Shia Imami Ismaili Muslim community is a worldwide religious community that arrived in Portugal with migrants, mostly from Mozambique, where it has been settled since the middle of the eighteenth century.[14]

During the nineteenth century, the community intensified its active participation on international stages such as the League of Nations and the United Nations, nowadays through the Aga Khan Development Network. The Network was founded by His Highness the Aga Khan, the 49th Hereditary Imam (spiritual leader) of the Ismaili Muslims. It includes nine development agencies focusing on humanitarian, social, cultural and economic activity, mainly in Asia and Africa.[15]

The relationship between Portugal and the Ismaili Imamat was first regulated by the Protocol of Co-operation published on 15 March 2006. This Protocol establishes cooperation between the two parties in development in the

13 https://dre.pt/web/guest/legislacao-consolidada/-/lc/106639383/202005061452/73413175/diploma/indice, last accessed on 5 May 2020.

14 Vadil, AbdoolKarim, "Comunidade Islâmica em Portugal", in *Dicionário Temático da Lusofonia*, Cristovão, Fernando (org.), (Lisbon: Associação de Cultura Lusófona—Texto Editores, 2005).

15 Canotilho, Machado, "Metódica Multinível", p. 268.

social, cultural and economic fields through the Aga Khan Development Network (AKDN). In 2009, an agreement resulting in the implementation of Chapter V of the Religious Freedom Act was established by Portugal and the Ismaili Imamat. The agreement states that the Ismaili Imamat can create and maintain religious schools and ecclesiastical culture without any monitoring by or supervision from the Portuguese state. Article 6 determines that within its freedom of teaching, this religious community has the right to create and direct non-religious schools at all teaching levels, within the parameters defined by Portuguese law. It sanctions the activity in Portugal of the Aga Khan University, the University of Central Asia and the Institute of Ismaili Studies and other educational institutions or organs under the aegis and control of the Ismaili Imamat. The only condition imposed on the conducting of these activities is respect for Portuguese law relating to the status of the institution.

The agreement also determines the regime for the designation of representatives to the Commission on Religious Freedom and the Commission for the Religious Persuasions' Broadcasting Time. In both situations, a member of the community is nominated by the Minister of Justice and the Government, respectively (article 7).

Article 56 of the Religious Freedom Act gives us the framework of the composition and operation of the Commission on Religious Freedom.[16] This Commission is composed of the Chairman, two members appointed by the Portuguese Episcopal Conference and three members appointed by the Minister of Justice from among persons put forward by churches and non-Catholic religious communities settled in Portugal and by federations in which they are integrated. This nomination must respect the principle of tolerance. What happens in article 7 of the Agreement between Portugal and the Ismaili Imamat is the fast-tracking of the statute that this religious community would have after 30 years of organised social presence in Portugal (article 37 (2) of the Religious Freedom Act). This provision does not always guarantee a seat on the Commission on Religious Freedom.

The Commission for the Religious Persuasions' Broadcasting Time[17] exists to allocate and distribute broadcasting time for churches and other registered religious communities, as set out in article 25 of the Religious Freedom Act. In the same way as for the Commission on Religious Freedom discussed above, the organ is composed of representatives of the Catholic Church and Churches and other religious communities settled in the country or the federations in which

16 See below—3.3. Commission on Religious Freedom.

17 See below—3.4. Commission for the Religious Persuasions Broadcasting Time.

they are integrated. The agreement between Portugal and the Ismaili Imamat, yet again, speeds up the process for this religious community. In 2015, a historic agreement to establish the Global Seat of the Imamat Ismaili in Portugal was signed, straightening the cooperation and relationship between both parties.[18]

We note that the agreed relationship between the Portuguese Republic and Ismaili Imamat could exist without this formal document. The Portuguese Religious Freedom Act underlines the equality between churches and religious communities by considering a vast number of collective religious rights.

18 https://dre.pt/web/guest/pesquisa/-/search/70819827/details/normal?q=imamat+ismaili, last accessed on 16 November 2020.

CHAPTER 3

State Support for Islamic Religious Communities

The state's support for religious communities is also defined in the Religious Freedom Act. As stated above, there is no distinction between the statute and the rights of the different churches and religious communities in Portugal. Therefore, we will analyse the support that the Portuguese state gives to the different churches and religious communities, guaranteeing their collective religious rights, which also include those of Islamic communities.

3.1 Religious Property or Use of Property for Religious Ends

One of the collective rights that are crucial for a religious community is the ability to have a headquarters, a physical place where the community can meet and organise its rites. How this can come about differs. On one hand, the community can rent a building or part of a building to use as headquarters or a place of worship (this option is summarised in article 29); on the other hand, churches and religious communities can own such buildings, which also benefit from special regulations provided in article 30 of the Religious Freedom Act.

As regards the use of property for religious purposes, when the property is intended for other purposes this should be agreed upon by the landlord, or, in the case of a condominium (apartment blocks with different apartment owners), by the majority of the condominium owners, as set out in article 29.

> Artigo 29.º—Utilização para fins religiosos de prédios destinados a outros fins[1]
> 1—Havendo acordo do proprietário, ou da maioria dos condóminos no caso de edifício em propriedade horizontal, a utilização para fins religiosos do prédio ou da fração destinados a outros fins não pode ser fundamento de objeção, nem da aplicação de sanções, pelas autoridades administrativas ou autárquicas, enquanto não existir uma alternativa adequada à realização dos mesmos fins.

1 https://dre.pt/web/guest/legislacao-consolidada/-/lc/106639383/202005061652/73413244/diploma/indice, last accessed on 5 May 2020.

2—O disposto no n.º 1 não prejudica os direitos dos condóminos recorrerem a juízo nos termos gerais.

The legal text also provides that this use cannot be the basis of an objection, or for the application of penalties by administrative city authorities, if there is no suitable alternative for achieving this objective. Consequently, this is an exception to the general regime about the use of Portuguese property. The use of buildings or parts of property for religious ends does not require a special permit.

In the case of a condominium, the requirement that the majority of the condominium owners agree is intended to prevent one or a few residents from objecting to the religious use of the relevant part of the property just out of simple prejudice, discrimination or arbitrariness, without invoking any basis related to disturbance in the quality of life, or knowingly being tempted to abuse their right of veto and trying to extract bribes from the religious community concerned in exchange for their authorisation.[2] However, it should be borne in mind that if a religious community violates the rights of residents in the condominium by allowing too many people to use it or making too much noise, the residents can always resort to urgent proceedings to protect those rights provided for in Article 878 of the Code of Civil Procedure, where it is said that a court 'may be required to enact specific measures to avoid the consummation of any unlawful and direct threat to the physical or moral personality of a human being or to mitigate, or to end, the effects of an offence already committed.' The objective of the Constitution and the law is always to achieve a reasonable and proportional balance between the various fundamental rights where there is a collision between them, making possible the practical agreement, harmonisation and maximum effectiveness of the rights and interests at stake, without totally privileging one to the detriment of others.

Religious communities may be concerned primarily with immaterial and spiritual reality, but they are made up of physical beings living in a material world. Tangible real property is also important for religious communities. Portuguese law is well aware of that. We can find specific regulation of religious assets in Article 30. No place of worship, building, annexe or objects of worship can be demolished or used for any other purpose. This is the general rule that can be overturned by a prior agreement with the church or religious community; by expropriation for public use or by requisition; in case of urgent public

2 Valente, David, Franco, Alberto, *Liberdade Religiosa—Nova Lei, Anotada e Comentada* (Lisbon: Dislivro, 2003), p. 52.

need; or when the demolition is necessary because the building is likely to collapse or represents a danger to public health. The principle of proportionality should govern any public action taken in this respect.

Artigo 30.º—Bens religiosos[3]
1—Nenhum templo, edifício, dependência ou objeto do culto pode ser demolido ou destinado a outro fim, a não ser por acordo prévio com a respetiva igreja ou comunidade religiosa, por expropriação por utilidade pública ou por requisição, em caso de urgente necessidade pública, salvo quando a demolição se torne necessária por a construção ameaçar ruína ou oferecer perigo para a saúde pública.
2—Nos casos de expropriação, de requisição e de demolição referidos no número anterior, é ouvida, sempre que possível, a respetiva igreja ou comunidade religiosa. Esta tem igualmente direito de audição prévia na determinação da execução de obras necessárias para corrigir más condições de salubridade, solidez ou segurança contra o risco de incêndio e na classificação de bens religiosos como de valor cultural.
3—Em qualquer caso, não será praticado ato algum de apropriação ou de utilização não religiosa sem que previamente os bens tenham sido privados da sua natureza religiosa pela respetiva igreja ou comunidade religiosa.

The church or the religious community is heard whenever possible when there is a decision to proceed with the expropriation, requisition or demolition. It should also be heard before the decision is made so that it can take action to ameliorate the asset's conditions or to have the religious assets classed as cultural values. Public authority measures that may be taken in this area are subject to the fundamental rights of prior hearing and due process.

The Act also ensures that the appropriation or non-religious use of the asset will not be carried out without the church or religious community first surrendering it as a religious asset (article 30 (3)).

3 https://dre.pt/web/guest/legislacao-consolidada/-/lc/106639383/202005061752/73413245/diploma/indice, last accessed on 5 May 2020.

3.2 Tax Benefits

Tax benefits for religious entities have existed since the time of the monarchy, considering that the monarch's power was based on divine right and there was a very straightforward relationship between the Church and the Crown, even regarding property. It must be remembered that the presence of religious communities (i.e. Christianity, Judaism and Islam) in Portugal predates the creation of the Portuguese state itself, in 1143, at the time of the so-called Christian reconquest of the Iberian Peninsula. For this reason, political, patrimonial and fiscal conflicts between the state and religious denominations, and especially the Catholic Church, have been a constant throughout the history of Portugal. In today's secular, constitutional state fiscal regulations ought to apply equally to any church or religious community that is qualified as such by the rules set out by Portuguese legislation and regulation.[4]

Article 31 of the Religious Freedom Act starts by defining tax-free contributions. Every registered church or religious community is exempt from any taxation on donations by its members directed towards religious purposes (article 31 (1a)); donations made by the general public collected inside or at the door of places of worship, or in buildings owned by the church or religious community (article 31 (1b)). Registered religious communities and churches can also freely disseminate declarations, notices and instructions on religious matters on places of worship without paying any fees or taxes (article 31 (1c)).

> Artigo 31.º—Prestações livres de impostos[5]
> 1—As igrejas e demais comunidades religiosas podem livremente, sem estarem sujeitas a qualquer imposto:
> a) Receber prestações dos crentes para o exercício do culto e ritos, bem como donativos para a realização dos seus fins religiosos, com carácter regular ou eventual;
> b) Fazer coletas públicas, designadamente dentro ou à porta dos lugares de culto, assim como dos edifícios ou lugares que lhes pertençam;
> c) Distribuir gratuitamente publicações com declarações, avisos ou instruções em matéria religiosa e afixá-las nos lugares de culto.

Number 2 clarifies the exceptions to this "freedom from taxation" rule expressed in number 1 of article 31. Registered churches and religious communi-

4 Machado, *Liberdade religiosa*, pp. 371–372.

5 https://dre.pt/web/guest/legislacao-consolidada/-/lc/106639383/202005061852/73413246/diploma/indice, last accessed on 5 May 2020.

ties are obliged to pay the taxes and fees due when offering corporate services on training, therapy and spiritual counselling.

> 2—Não está abrangido pelo disposto no número anterior o preço de prestações de formação, terapia ou aconselhamento espiritual, oferecidas empresarialmente.

Article 32 of the Religious Freedom Act lists all the fiscal benefits that religious entities are eligible for. Number 1 sets out the exemption, applying to all registered religious collective entities, from taxes and general, regional or local contributions that concern places of worship and buildings where they are directly intended for the achievement of religious activities (paragraph a); for installations which are of direct and exclusive support for religious activities (paragraph b); to seminaries and other institutions that aim to train ministers of religion and teachers of religious education (paragraph c); outbuildings or annexes of the abovementioned properties that are intended to be used for special social welfare work (paragraph d); and gardens and parks of the properties referred to as long as they are not intended to be used for profit (paragraph e).

> Artigo 32.º—Benefícios fiscais[6]
> 1—As pessoas coletivas religiosas inscritas estão isentas de qualquer imposto ou contribuição geral, regional ou local, sobre:
> a) Os lugares de culto ou outros prédios ou partes deles diretamente destinados à realização de fins religiosos;
> b) As instalações de apoio direto e exclusivo às atividades com fins religiosos;
> c) Os seminários ou quaisquer estabelecimentos efetivamente destinados à formação dos ministros do culto ou ao ensino da religião;
> d) As dependências ou anexos dos prédios descritos nas alíneas a) a c) a uso de instituições particulares de solidariedade social;
> e) Os jardins e logradouros dos prédios descritos nas alíneas a) a d) desde que não estejam destinados a fins lucrativos.

Number 2 of article 32 exempts registered religious collective entities from taxes imposed on assets such as the municipal "SISA" tax and taxes on inheritances and donations. The "SISA" municipal tax was replaced in 2004 by the

6 https://dre.pt/web/guest/legislacao-consolidada/-/lc/106639383/202005061952/73413247/diploma/indice, last accessed on 5 May 2020.

Municipal Tax on Transfers of Real Property, and the specific tax on inheritances and donations was also abolished by the same Executive Legislative Decree.[7] Taking into account the exemption from any taxes that concern assets, article 32(2) is the legal basis that today exempts churches and religious communities from Stamp Duty[8] which is charged on every deed, document, contract, paper or other fact determined by the law which concerns transfers for value or property and also transactions as gifts.

> 2—As pessoas coletivas religiosas inscritas estão igualmente isentas do imposto municipal de sisa e sobre as sucessões e doações ou quaisquer outros com incidência patrimonial substitutivos destes, quanto:
> a) Às aquisições de bens para fins religiosos;
> b) Aos atos de instituição de fundações, uma vez inscritas como pessoas coletivas religiosas.

The definition of religious activity or religious purpose is therefore of fundamental importance in tax matters. Religious communities cannot claim tax benefits for properties or activities that are not strictly religious. For example, if a religious confession leases some of its lands to a commercial company, it cannot claim exemption from municipal property tax. Likewise, if the leadership of a religious confession has direct access to its bank accounts and uses the money deposited there to pay for its personal expenses, or receives abnormal and disproportionately high remuneration, the tax authority can requalify the religious confession and treat it as a company, even if only for tax purposes.

Article 32 also provides fiscal benefits for individuals on donations made in favour of churches or religious communities.

Donations to registered religious entities are encouraged by a fiscal benefit granted to the donors in their income tax. These donations are deductible at 25 per cent of the amount of the income taxed. Through the years, article 32 (3) has been updated. Initially, in 2001, the limitation was set at 25 per cent of the donation, up to 15 per cent of the assessment of income taxed. In 2009, the relevant amount for calculating the 25 per cent deduction was the value of 130 per cent of the donation, the limits remained the same referring to their stipulation

7 ELD no. 287/2003, available at https://dre.pt/web/guest/legislacao-consolidada/-/lc/34499575/view?q=decreto+lei+287%2F2003, last accessed on 5 May 2020.

8 Imposto Selo—regulated by Law no. 150/99, available in https://dre.pt/web/guest/legislacao-consolidada/-/lc/34540175/view?q=C%C3%B3digo+do+Imposto+de+Selo, last accessed on 5 May 2020.

in the Fiscal Benefits Statute.[9] Thus, the state recognises, in accordance with the principle of cooperation, that religious denominations are important partners, within civil society, for the achievement of important purposes of human development and social integration.

> 3—Os donativos atribuídos pelas pessoas singulares às pessoas coletivas religiosas inscritas para efeitos de imposto sobre o rendimento das pessoas singulares são dedutíveis à coleta, nos termos e limites fixados nas alíneas b) e c) do n.º 1 do artigo 63.º do Estatuto dos Benefícios Fiscais, sendo a sua importância considerada em 130 % do seu quantitativo.

Regarding income tax, Portuguese taxpayers can allocate 0.5 per cent of their paid income tax to specific institutions and entities. It must be stressed that this is not a religious tax, required by religious confessions from their faithful, or a mandatory donation, structured by the state in favour of religious confessions. We are dealing here to a certain extent with the logic of participatory social rights budgeting. As we will see, taxpayers have the option to allocate 0.5 per cent of their income tax to their own religious community or to any private entity engaged in activities of a social, cultural or artistic nature, included in a list accessible to the public on the tax authority website. The money so earmarked is subsequently distributed by the state to the entities designated by the taxpayers. It is worth paying attention to the details of this arrangement.

Entities with religious objectives or charities, churches or religious communities settled in the country are eligible to receive these donations. In their annual tax returns taxpayers indicate what entity they would like to send the donation to. The regime is set out in numbers 4, 5, 6 and 7 of article 32. This benefit is available only to settled religious communities and churches.

> 4—Uma quota equivalente a 0,5 % do imposto sobre o rendimento das pessoas singulares, liquidado com base nas declarações anuais, pode ser destinada pelo contribuinte, para fins religiosos ou de beneficência, a uma igreja ou comunidade religiosa radicada no País, que indicará na declaração de rendimentos, desde que essa igreja ou comunidade religiosa tenha requerido o benefício fiscal.

9 ELD no. 215/89, updated by Law no. 71/2018, available at https://dre.pt/web/guest/legislacao-consolidada/-/lc/120267084/202001141708/73682261/diploma/indice?q=estatuto+dos+benef%C3%ADcios+fiscais, last accessed on 5 May 2020.

> 5—As verbas destinadas, nos termos do número anterior, às igrejas e comunidades religiosas são entregues pelo Tesouro às mesmas ou às suas organizações representativas, que apresentarão na Direcção-Geral dos Impostos relatório anual do destino dado aos montantes recebidos.
> 6—O contribuinte que não use a faculdade prevista no n.º 4 pode fazer uma consignação fiscal equivalente a favor de uma pessoa coletiva de utilidade pública de fins de beneficência ou de assistência ou humanitários ou de uma instituição particular de solidariedade social, que indicará na sua declaração de rendimentos.
> 7—As verbas a entregar às entidades referidas nos n.ºs 4 e 6 devem ser inscritas em rubrica própria no Orçamento do Estado.

After the tax has been assessed and been paid by the taxpayers, the amount is delivered by the Treasury to the churches or religious communities which are required to publish a report stating the destination of the amount received (number 5).

If taxpayers do not wish to attribute their 0.5 per cent of income tax to a church or religious entity (as set out in number 4), they can do so in favour of a collective entity of public utility for charity, assistance or humanitarian purposes or a private social welfare institution, by nominating it in their income tax returns (number 6).

Article 79-F of the Personal Income Tax Code[10] provides for a tax deduction of 15 per cent of the VAT attributed to each member of the household, up to a limit of €250, calculated on the basis of invoices issued for services purchased, allowing this amount to be allocated to the religious community to which the taxpayer has decided to allocate the 0.5 per cent of tax.

The final numbers of article 32 of the Religious Freedom Act were introduced in 2010, in the Act that approved the 2010 State Budget. Number 8 introduced the state's obligation to publish online a list of every entity eligible to receive the fiscally assigned amounts that were provided for in numbers 4 and 6. Since 2010, the entity the taxpayer wishes to assign the amount to is specified in the annual return (number 9). Number 10 specifies a deadline of 31 of March of the year after the delivery of the return for the amount to be sent by the Treasury to the relevant entities.

10 The original text is available in https://dre.pt/web/guest/legislacao-consolidada/-/lc/131552179/202005051135/73807635/diploma/indice?q=c%C3%B3digo+do+imposto+do+rendimento+singulares, last accessed on 5 May 2020.

8—A administração fiscal publica, na página das declarações eletrónicas, até ao 1.º dia do prazo de entrega das declarações, previsto no artigo 60.º, todas as entidades que se encontram em condições de beneficiar das consignações fiscais previstas nos n.ºs 4 e 6.
9—Da nota demonstrativa da liquidação de IRS deve constar a identificação da entidade beneficiada, bem como o montante consignado nos termos dos n.ºs 4 e 6.
10—As verbas referidas nos n.ºs 4 e 6, respeitantes a imposto sobre o rendimento das pessoas singulares liquidado com base nas declarações de rendimentos entregues dentro do prazo legal, devem ser transferidas para as entidades beneficiárias até 31 de março do ano seguinte à da entrega da referida declaração.

A report of 2019 revealed that in 2018 the donations to churches and religious entities increased as compared to 2017, amounting to a total of €164,137,584.92, compared to €42,915,345.66 in the previous year.[11] This reveals that this system was well accepted and that it is working well within the framework of a democratic, open and pluralist society. It also demonstrates that citizens believe that the system just described, in addition to giving them an important right to budgetary participation, provides for a good balance between the principles of freedom, equality and cooperation, which are so important in the relationship between religious denominations and the state.

Structurally, articles 31 and 32 are in Chapter III of the Religious Freedom Act which regulates the "Collective Right to Religious Freedom". Analysing the Act further we find in Chapter VIII—"Supplementary and temporary provisions" (the final chapter)—article 65 which exempts settled churches and religious communities from value added tax. This is an added fiscal benefit, though intended as temporary, which differentiates settled churches from registered churches and communities' benefits.

There was a need to improve and update the regulation on exemption from value added tax in accordance with the European Union's regulations. The previous Executive Legislative Decree that regulated this exemption (ELD no. 20/90, of 30 January[12]) violated the European Union's directive on value

11 The report entitled "Benefícios Fiscais em Portugal—conceitos, metodologia e prática" was commissioned by the Ministry of Finances from the Working Group for the Study of Fiscal Benefits. The Working Group was created by Order no. 4222/2018, available at https://www.portugal.gov.pt/download-ficheiros/ficheiro.aspx?v=1448be63-5771-4fe2-96bb-489648338726, last accessed on 5 May 2020.

12 The current version is available at https://dre.pt/web/guest/pesquisa/-/search/333523/details/normal?q=Decreto+Lei+20%2F90, last accessed on 5 May 2020.

added tax (VAT Directive 77/388/EEC[13]). This earlier provision allowed the devolution of VAT to the Catholic Church and to the private social security institutions it owned, an amount which (in)directly financed its activity. This regime was applicable only to the Catholic Church and its institutions, as set out in the 1940s Concordat. This was a violation of the principle of equality of the fiscal system and of the principle of the non-confessional state.[14]

So, in order to correct this functional inequality, the legislator inserted into the Act the ability of all settled churches and religious communities, their institutions, associations and foundations to choose between two regimes. This is the proposition set out in article 65. Religious entities can now choose between the restitution of VAT, until 2001 only beneficial to the Catholic Church, or the benefit of the 0.5 per cent of income tax previously referred to in article 32.

This ability to opt for different regimes was inserted as a mechanism to minimise the impact of the complete withdrawal of this benefit. This analysis allows us to understand why this provision was inserted in the chapter on temporary provisions. The legislator is required (as is intended in the Ministry of Justice's draft Bill) to revoke this exemption in the future.[15]

19 years since the approval of the law, the Executive Legislative Decree no. 20/90, of 13 of January is still in force. Settled religious communities and churches can still choose between either regime.

> Artigo 65.º—Isenção do imposto sobre o valor acrescentado[16]
> 1—As igrejas e comunidades religiosas radicadas no País, os institutos de vida consagrada e outros institutos com a natureza de associações ou fundações por aquelas fundados ou reconhecidos, e ainda as federações e as associações em que as mesmas se integrem, podem optar pelo regime previsto no n.º 1 do Artigo 1.º do Decreto-Lei n.º 20/90, de 13 de Janeiro, alterado pela Lei n.º 52-C/96, de 27 de Dezembro, pelo Decreto-Lei n.º 323/98, de 30 de Outubro, pela Lei n.º 30-C/2000, de 29 de Dezembro, e pelo Decreto-Lei n.º 238/2006, de 20 de Dezembro, enquanto vigorar, não se lhes aplicando, nesse caso, o n.º 4 do Artigo 32.º da presente lei.

13 Current version and modification history available at https://eur-lex.europa.eu/legal-content/EN/ALL/?uri=CELEX:31977L0388, last accessed on 5 May 2020.

14 Ministry of Justice, *Proposta de Lei apresentada à Assembleia da República*, (Lisbon: Ministério da Justiça, 1999), p. 57.

15 Ministry of Justice, *Proposta de Lei apresentada à Assembleia da República*, (Lisbon: Ministério da Justiça, 1999), p. 61.

16 https://dre.pt/web/guest/legislacao-consolidada/-/lc/106639383/202005062152/73413285/diploma/indice, last accessed on 5 May 2020.

3.3 Commission on Religious Freedom

State support for the different churches and religious communities, Islamic communities included, goes beyond benefits related to estates and taxes. In the Religious Freedom Act the legislator saw the need to set up the Commission on Religious Freedom. This is an advisory body that develops studies, information, issues opinions and proposes changes in all matters concerning freedom of religion in Portugal. The Commission's chairman and members took office for the first time on 17 March 2004. Since then, it has proven to be a very important regulatory tool. Underlying this entity, we can find a logic of combining hetero-regulation with self-regulation. While it monitors the religious situation, studying its dynamics over time, it gives religious confessions a platform for participatory interaction in the regulation of religious activity according to constitutional principles.

Chapter VI provides for its creation (article 52), its functions (article 53), its mandate (article 54), cooperation with departments and public bodies (article 55), its composition and operation (article 56) and the functions of the Chairman (article 57).

> Artigo 53.º—Funções[17]
> 1—A Comissão tem funções de estudo, informação, parecer e proposta em todas as matérias relacionadas com a aplicação da Lei de Liberdade Religiosa, com o desenvolvimento, melhoria e eventual revisão da mesma lei e, em geral, com o direito das religiões em Portugal.
> 2—A Comissão tem igualmente funções de investigação científica das igrejas, comunidades e movimentos religiosos em Portugal.

As regards competences, article 54 assigns the Commission on Religious Freedom the task of issuing opinions on various matters, such as agreements between churches and religious communities and the Portuguese state (point a); churches and religious communities' settlement certifications (point b); the composition of the Commission for the Religious Persuasions' Broadcasting Time[18] (point c); applications for registration of churches and religious communities (point d). The Commission is also to develop studies on the evolution of religious movements in Portugal, gather and keep up to date information about those movements and provide scientific and statistical information to

17 https://dre.pt/web/guest/legislacao-consolidada/-/lc/106639383/202005062352/73413271/diploma/indice, last accessed on 5 May 2020.

18 See below—3.4 Commission for the Religious Persuasions' Broadcasting Time.

the services, institutions or people interested in the subject (point e). An annual report is published about the Commission's activities.[19]

The Commission is also called upon to issue studies, information, opinions and proposals whenever asked to do so by the Assembly of the Republic, the Government, or by its own decision (point f). It is to develop its internal regulation (number 2).

> Artigo 54.º—Competência[20]
> 1—No exercício das suas funções compete, nomeadamente, à Comissão:
> a) Emitir parecer sobre os projetos de acordos entre igrejas ou comunidades religiosas e o Estado;
> b) Emitir parecer sobre a radicação no País de igrejas ou comunidades religiosas;
> c) Emitir parecer sobre a composição da Comissão do Tempo de Emissão das Confissões Religiosas;
> d) Emitir os pareceres sobre a inscrição de igrejas ou comunidades religiosas que forem requeridos pelo serviço do registo das pessoas coletivas religiosas;
> e) Estudar a evolução dos movimentos religiosos em Portugal e, em especial, reunir e manter atualizada a informação sobre novos movimentos religiosos, fornecer a informação científica e estatística necessária aos serviços, instituições e pessoas interessadas e publicar um relatório anual sobre a matéria;
> f) Elaborar estudos, informações, pareceres e propostas que lhe forem cometidos por lei, pela Assembleia da República, pelo Governo ou por própria iniciativa.
> 2—A Comissão elabora o seu próprio regulamento interno.

The Commission is composed of the Chairman (designated by the Council of Ministers, with a three-year mandate, with the possibility of renewal[21]); two

19 Activities reports are available here: http://www.clr.mj.pt/sections/agenda/relatorio-de-actividades.

20 https://dre.pt/web/guest/legislacao-consolidada/-/lc/106639383/202005070052/73413272/diploma/indice, last accessed on 5 May 2020.

21 The position of the Chairman is regulated by article 57. It specifies that the Chairman should be chosen from among jurists of acknowledged competence, sets out the possibility of the functions being carried out simultaneously while working exclusively in a teaching position. The function of the Chairman is perceived as legal scientific investigation.

members designated by the Portuguese Episcopal Conference;[22] three members designated by the Government from among those nominated by the non-Catholic churches and communities with regard to representation and the principles of tolerance. The remaining five members are also designated by the Government from among recognised specialists with scientific competence in order to ensure the plurality and neutrality of the state in religious matters (article 56 (1)).

> Artigo 56.º—Composição e funcionamento[23]
> 1—A Comissão é constituída pelas pessoas agrupadas nas duas alíneas seguintes:
> a) O presidente, dois membros designados pela Conferência Episcopal Portuguesa e três membros designados pelo membro do Governo competente na área da justiça de entre as pessoas indicadas pelas igrejas ou comunidades religiosas não católicas radicadas no País e pelas federações em que as mesmas se integrem, tendo em consideração a representatividade de cada uma e o princípio da tolerância;
> b) Cinco pessoas de reconhecida competência científica nas áreas relativas às funções da Comissão designadas pelo membro do Governo competente na área da justiça, de modo a assegurar o pluralismo e a neutralidade do Estado em matéria religiosa.
> 2—Terão assento na Comissão, sempre que esta o entender necessário ou conveniente, representantes governamentais nas áreas da justiça, das finanças, da administração interna e do trabalho e solidariedade designados a título permanente, que não terão direito a voto.
> 3—Quando a questão sob apreciação diga respeito a ministério diferente dos indicados no n.º 2, pode participar nas sessões correspondentes um representante do ministério em causa.
> 4—O mandato dos membros da Comissão é trienal e poderá ser renovado.
> 5—Os membros da Comissão têm o direito de fazer lavrar voto de vencido nos pareceres referidos nas alíneas a), b), c) e d) do artigo 54.º, quando tenham participado na deliberação que os aprovou.

22 The body that joins the bishops of the Catholic Church in Portugal. http://www.conferenciaepiscopal.pt/v1/.

23 https://dre.pt/web/guest/legislacao-consolidada/-/lc/106639383/202005070252/73413274/diploma/indice, last accessed on 5 May 2020.

6—A Comissão pode funcionar em plenário ou em comissão permanente.

Whenever the Commission finds the need, members of the Government in the areas of Justice, Finance, Internal Affairs and Work and Solidarity can sit in the Commission on a permanent basis, but without the right to vote. If a question arises that concerns other Ministries, a representative can also participate in the Commission's session that deals with the issue (article 56 (2) (3)).

The members are appointed for three-year terms which can be renewed (article 52 (4)). Whenever there is an opinion to be issued (article 54), the members of the Commission have the right to cast dissenting votes, as the members were part of the plenary or the permanent committee that decided on the subject (article 52 (5) (6)).

Following its formation, the Commission was chaired by Mr José Manuel Menéres Sampaio Pimentel (2004–2006) and Mr Mario Soares (2007–2016). The current chairman Mr José Eduardo Vera Cruz Jardim took office in 2016. It is worth emphasising that each of them has done an excellent job in this area, their conduct having always been characterised by great humanity, sensitivity and common sense.

The positive atmosphere that exists between the various religious denominations is reflected in the public sphere. For example, when there are discussions in Portuguese society about fracturing ethical issues (e.g. abortion, euthanasia), it is common for the various religious denominations to come together to present a common position.

The Islamic Community has been represented on the Commission since the beginning, with the designation of Mr Abdool Magid Karim Vakil, representing Lisbon's Islamic Community, and Mr Nazim Ahmad, representing the Aga Khan Network of Development. In 2016, when the mandate was renewed Mr Rahim Firozali stepped in as a member of the Commission representing the National Council of the Islamic Ismaili community, which he chairs.[24]

24 Order no. 10786/2016 of the Minister of Justice nominating the members of the Commission on Religious Freedom, available at http://www.clr.mj.pt/sections/comissao/3-mandato-5-9-2016/tomada-de-posse-dos-senhores-presidente-membros-clr-5set2016/downloadFile/attachedFile_f0/despacho_nomeacao_dos_membros_2016.pdf, last accessed on 5 May 2020.

3.4 Commission for the Religious Persuasions' Broadcasting Time

The Commission for the Religious Persuasions' Broadcasting Time was also created by the Religious Freedom Act. The Portuguese Constitution grants churches and religious communities the right to use their own media to pursue their activities (Article 41 (5) of the Portuguese Constitution). They also benefit from the constitutional right to broadcast on the radio and television public broadcasting service, a right which is granted in Article 40 (1) of the Portuguese Constitution to "social organisations with national scope".[25]

Article 25 of the Religious Freedom Act regulates how the broadcasting time for each registered church and religious community is decided upon. The entities themselves are responsible for the contents of their broadcasting times (article 25 (1)). The distribution of those times are decided by agreement between the Commission and the companies that own television and radio public broadcasting services, taking account of the sizes of the different religious confessions and the tolerance principle (article 25 (2)).

The Commission is composed of representatives of the Catholic Church and of the registered churches and religious communities. Such representatives are appointed for three-year periods by the Minister of Justice and Minister of Culture, on the recommendation of the Commission on Religious Freedom (article 25 (3)).

> Artigo 25.º—Tempos de emissão religiosa[26]
> 1—Nos serviços públicos de televisão e de radiodifusão é garantido às igrejas e demais comunidades religiosas inscritas, por si, através da respetiva organização representativa, ou conjuntamente, quando preferirem participar como se fossem uma única confissão, um tempo de emissão, fixado globalmente para todas, para prossecução dos seus fins religiosos.
> 2—A atribuição e distribuição do tempo de emissão referido no número anterior é feita tendo em conta a representatividade das respetivas confissões e o princípio da tolerância, por meio de acordos entre a Comissão do Tempo de Emissão das Confissões Religiosas e as empresas titulares dos serviços públicos de televisão e de radiodifusão.
> 3—A Comissão do Tempo de Emissão das Confissões Religiosas é constituída por representantes da Igreja Católica e das igrejas e comunidades religiosas radicadas no País ou das federações em que as mesmas se

25 Canotilho, Moreira, *Constituição da República*, p. 616.

26 https://dre.pt/web/guest/legislacao-consolidada/-/lc/106639383/202005070452/73413240/diploma/indice, last accessed on 5 May 2020.

integrem, designados por três anos por despacho conjunto dos membros do Governo responsáveis pelas áreas da justiça e da comunicação social, depois de ouvida a Comissão da Liberdade Religiosa.

Since 2018,[27] the Commission has been composed of seven members, each representing a different church or religious community registered in Portugal. Lisbon's Islamic Community is represented by Mr Mahomed Abed Gulamo, the only representative of Islam on the Commission.

The time allocated to each church or religious community is broadcast daily in the programme "Fé dos Homens" (Man's Faith) on channel 2 of the public television broadcaster. In 2009, the programme started to be broadcast also on the public radio service. "Fé dos Homens" includes the promotion of activities of the 14 legally recognised religious confessions in Portugal.[28]

Churches and religious activities can also be promoted weekly, in the programme "Caminhos" (Pathways), also broadcast on channel 2 of the public television service.

27 Through joint order of the Minister of Justice and Minister of Culture, Order no. 7727/2018, of 13 of August, available here https://dre.pt/web/guest/pesquisa/-/search/115991761/details/normal?q=Despacho+7727%2F2018.

28 "Emissão inter-religiosa assinala domingo início de "A Fé dos Homens" na RDP" [Interreligious emmission stars on Sundays with the beginning of "Faith of Man" in RDP], available at https://www.rtp.pt/noticias/cultura/emissao-inter-religiosa-assinala-domingo-inicio-de-a-fe-dos-homens-na-rdp_n291453, last accessed on 5 May 2020.

CHAPTER 4

Muslims in Integration Law

The 1976 Portuguese Constitution sets out the principles of equality and universality as the basis of its bill of rights. There is no specific Act in the Portuguese legal system which includes Muslims.

> Artigo 12.º—Princípio da Universalidade[1]
> 1—Todos os cidadãos gozam dos direitos e estão sujeitos aos deveres consignados na Constituição.
> 2—As pessoas coletivas gozam dos direitos e estão sujeitas aos deveres compatíveis com a sua natureza.

The universality principle requires that every citizen enjoy their rights just as they are obliged to carry out the duties or obligations attached to them. Article 12 (2) applies the principle of universality to legal persons, which can enjoy rights and fulfil obligations only insofar as they are compatible with their juridical nature.

> Artigo 13.º—Princípio da igualdade[2]
> 1—Todos os cidadãos têm a mesma dignidade social e são iguais perante a lei.
> 2—Ninguém poder ser privilegiado, beneficiado, prejudicado, privado de qualquer direito ou isento de qualquer dever em razão da ascendência, sexo, raça, língua, território de origem, religião, convicções políticas ou ideológicas, instrução, situação económica, condição social ou orientação sexual.

Article 13 confirms the equality principle, specifying that everyone has the same social dignity before the law. It also states that no one can be privileged, benefited or harmed by or deprived of their rights, laying down a series of grounds that cannot be taken into account for a differentiated treatment by the law. Religion and political and ideological belief cannot be grounds for beneficial

1 https://dre.pt/web/guest/legislacao-consolidada/-/lc/337/202005051237/127969/diploma/indice, last accessed on 5 May 2020.

2 https://dre.pt/web/guest/legislacao-consolidada/-/lc/337/202005051337/127970/diploma/indice, last accessed on 5 May 2020.

or prejudicial legal regimes according to this fundamental constitutional principle, inserted into Part I of the Constitution entitled "Fundamental Rights and Duties."

Considering the high percentage of Muslims in Portugal who are of immigrant origin it is also interesting to refer to Article 15 of the Constitution which sets out the regime regarding the rights and duties of foreigners, stateless persons and European citizens.

> Artigo 15.º—Estrangeiros, apátridas, cidadãos europeus[3]
> 1. Os estrangeiros e os apátridas que se encontrem ou residam em Portugal gozam dos direitos e estão sujeitos aos deveres do cidadão português.
> 2. Excetuam-se do disposto no número anterior os direitos políticos, o exercício das funções públicas que não tenham carácter predominantemente técnico e os direitos e deveres reservados pela Constituição e pela lei exclusivamente aos cidadãos portugueses.
> 3. Aos cidadãos dos Estados de língua portuguesa com residência permanente em Portugal são reconhecidos, nos termos da lei e em condições de reciprocidade, direitos não conferidos a estrangeiros, salvo o acesso aos cargos de Presidente da República, Presidente da Assembleia da República, Primeiro-Ministro, Presidentes dos tribunais supremos e o serviço nas Forças Armadas e na carreira diplomática.
> 4. A lei pode atribuir a estrangeiros residentes no território nacional, em condições de reciprocidade, capacidade eleitoral ativa e passiva para a eleição dos titulares de órgãos de autarquias locais.
> 5. A lei pode ainda atribuir, em condições de reciprocidade, aos cidadãos dos Estados-membros da União Europeia residentes em Portugal o direito de elegerem e serem eleitos Deputados ao Parlamento Europeu.

In this context it is important to note that all foreigners who are in the territory or live in Portugal enjoy the same rights as Portuguese citizens. They are also obliged to fulfil the duties that come attached to those rights (article 1).

There are exceptions to this levelling between regimes, specifically related to political rights and the exercise of public functions (article 2). There are also reciprocity regimes governing citizens of Portuguese-speaking countries living in Portugal (article 3), who can enjoy more rights except those granting access to the offices of President of the Republic, President of the Parliament,

3 https://dre.pt/web/guest/legislacao-consolidada/-/lc/337/202005051537/127972/diploma/indice, last accessed on 5 May 2020.

Prime Minister, President of the Supreme Courts, service in the armed forces and a diplomatic career. European citizens can, also considering reciprocity, elect and be elected as Portuguese Members of the European Parliament (article 5). Other foreigners can elect and be elected to local government (article 4).

The Portuguese Constitution does not distinguish between original citizens and naturalised citizens, so naturalised citizens cannot suffer any restriction of rights, except where such restriction is specifically laid down in the Constitution.[4]

4 We are referring to specific provisions, such as Article 122 of the Portuguese Constitution which states that the office of President of the Republic can be accessed only by citizens of Portuguese origin who are over 35 years old: Canotilho, J.J. Gomes, *Direito Constitucional e a Teoria da Constituição* (Coimbra: Almedina, 2003), p. 420.

CHAPTER 5

Mosques and Prayer Houses

As regards places of worship, the Religious Freedom Act introduces the ability to use for religious purposes property originally intended for other purposes. Article 29 allows this use when the owner of the building permits it or, in case of jointly-owned property, when the majority of the owners agree about the use of the building for religious purposes. It also protects religious communities from the charges that could be levied by the administrative or municipal authorities. Number 2 clarifies that, in the case of jointly-owned property, the agreement to its use for religious purposes by the owners does not mean that they restrict their rights to be heard in a court of law.

> Artigo 29.º—Utilização para fins religiosos de prédios destinados a outros fins[1]
> 1—Havendo acordo do proprietário, ou da maioria dos condóminos no caso de edifício em propriedade horizontal, a utilização para fins religiosos do prédio ou da fração destinados a outros fins não pode ser fundamento de objeção, nem da aplicação de sanções, pelas autoridades administrativas ou autárquicas, enquanto não existir uma alternativa adequada à realização dos mesmos fins.
> 2—O disposto no n.º 1 não prejudica os direitos dos condóminos recorrerem a juízo nos termos gerais.

In Portugal, Islamic communities benefit from this regime, renting or owning buildings that were not built specifically for religious purposes but are now used for such purposes.

There are several places of worship of the different Islamic communities spread throughout the country. In Lisbon and its surroundings there are eight mosques and 22 places of worship. In central Portugal there are two mosques (in Coimbra and in Viseu) and a room for worship in Leiria. In the north of the country there are two mosques and five places of worship. In Alentejo, the Islamic community meets in two mosques (Beja and Évora), and in the Algarve

1 https://dre.pt/web/guest/legislacao-consolidada/-/lc/106639383/202005070652/73413244/diploma/indice, last accessed on 5 May 2020.

(the southern part of Portugal) there are five mosques (Albufeira, Armação de Pêra, Monte Choro, Portimão, Olhão) and three places of worship. There is also one mosque in the autonomous region of Madeira.[2]

2 Information gathered from http://halal.pt/myihp/locais-de-culto/.

CHAPTER 6

Burial and Cemeteries

Funerary customs are an important part of every religious belief. Portugal has a strong Catholic matrix; therefore, public cemeteries are normally near Catholic churches, and administrative regulations about cemeteries are more likely to embrace Catholic tradition than any other religious funerary ritual.

Portuguese law states that everyone should be buried in a public cemetery and it is also mandatory that all corpses are buried in coffins made of wood or zinc (article 6 of ELD no. 411/98[1]).

In Portugal, the competence to administer cemeteries falls on municipalities and *freguesias* (civil parishes).[2] The management, preservation and cleaning of cemeteries are within the competence of local authorities as determined by Act no. 75/2013 as amended by Act no. 58/2018.

> Artigo 16.º—Competências materiais[3]
> 1—Compete à junta de freguesia:
> (…)
> gg) Conceder terrenos, nos cemitérios propriedade da freguesia, para jazigos, mausoléus e sepulturas perpétuas;
> hh) Gerir, conservar e promover a limpeza dos cemitérios propriedade da freguesia;
> (…)

Article 16 endows the *freguesias* (civil parishes) with the competence to manage, preserve and clean cemeteries if they are the owners of the asset (article 16 (1)). It also falls within the competence of these local authorities to grant land within the cemeteries to the citizens for vaults, mausoleums and graves. The criteria for this concession is usually determined by administrative regulations passed by the local authorities.

1 ELD no. 411/98, 30 of December, available at https://dre.pt/application/file/a/286007.

2 Municipalities (Municípios) and Freguesias are Portugal's local authorities. They are made up of local representatives who aim to promote the interests of the local population. "Artigo 235.º—Autarquias locais (…) 2—As autarquias locais são pessoas coletivas territoriais dotadas de órgãos representativos, que visam a prossecução de interesses próprios das populações respetivas."

3 Act no. 75/2013, of 12 September available at https://dre.pt/web/guest/legislacao-consolidada/-/lc/view?cid=116042207

It also falls upon the Mayor to grant land in a cemetery owned by the municipality for vaults, mausoleums and graves.

> Artigo 35.º—Competências do presidente da câmara municipal
> (…)
> 2—Compete ainda ao presidente da câmara municipal:
> (…)
> p) Conceder terrenos, nos cemitérios propriedade do município, para jazigos, mausoléus e sepulturas perpétuas.

As this regulation is within the competence of local authorities there are various criteria for the allocation of space.

The Religious Freedom Act is silent on the subject. ELD no. 411/98[4] of 30 December, which governs the law relating to the dead, considers the possibility of burial outside public cemeteries, when—and only if—there are special spaces reserved for a different confession or religious belief.

> Artigo 11.º—Locais de inumação
> 1—A inumação não pode ter lugar fora de cemitério público, devendo ser efetuada em sepultura, jazigo ou local de consumpção aeróbia de cadáveres.
> 2—São excecionalmente permitidos:
> (…)
> b) A inumação em locais especiais ou reservados a pessoas de determinadas categorias, nomeadamente de certa nacionalidade, confissão ou regra religiosa, para tal autorizados pela câmara municipal respetiva;

These special locations, where burial is allowed under the exception to the general rule, must be authorised by the local authority (municipality).

In Palmela, the municipal regulation on the organisation and management of the cemetery makes possible the allocation of private sections to a community on the basis of its religious belief.

> Artigo 9.º—Organização do espaço[5]
> (…)

4 ELD no. 411/98, 30 of December, available at https://dre.pt/application/file/a/286007, last accessed on 5 May 2020.

5 Palmela's Cemetery regulation is available at https://www.cm-palmela.pt/cmpalmela/uploads/document/file/2082/Edital_n._65_DAF-DAG_2008.pdf, last accessed on 5 May 2020.

2—A Câmara Municipal pode instituir talhões privativos em razão de crença religiosa, praxis mortuária específica ou outro motivo que se considere justificado.

In the Lisbon area, there are three cemeteries with special sections designated for the Islamic communities: Lumiar, Odivelas and Feijó. These sections were required by the Islamic communities so that they could organise the land according to their traditions. In the Islamic tradition, the positioning of the body is relevant—the right side of the body should face Mecca. The body can be carried in a coffin (as required by Portuguese law) but the body inside is shrouded in white cloth.

Usually, individuals are buried in public cemeteries in the area they lived in. This rule posed a problem for the Islamic community in the greater Lisbon area because not every public cemetery in those municipalities had a specific area for Muslims. Lisbon Municipality's Cemeteries Regulation (in Articles 3 and 4)[6] allows non-resident members of the Islamic community to be buried in the municipality's cemeteries.

6 Original document available in https://informacoeseservicos.lisboa.pt/fileadmin/downloadcenter/normativas/regulamentos/comercio/RCemiteriosM_Ed68_1984.pdf, last accessed on 7 October 2020.

CHAPTER 7

Education and Schools

To analyse education and Islam in Portugal we must first consider the freedoms to learn and to teach set out in Article 43 of the Portuguese Constitution.

Artigo 43.º—Liberdade de aprender e ensinar[1]
1. É garantida a liberdade de aprender e ensinar.
2. O Estado não pode programar a educação e a cultura segundo quaisquer diretrizes filosóficas, estéticas, políticas, ideológicas ou religiosas.
3. O ensino público não será confessional.
4. É garantido o direito de criação de escolas particulares e cooperativas.

The Portuguese Constitution guarantees the freedom to learn and to teach that must be provided by the State (article 1). At the same time, it says that the State may not lay down the syllabus for education and culture following any specific philosophical, aesthetic, political, ideological or religious directives (article 2).

Article 43 (3) was first introduced in the original text of the Constitution,[2] and states that public education shall not be linked to a religious belief. The Concordat of 1940, still in force at the time, between the Holy See and Portugal, ensured that public education should be guided by Christian doctrinal principals and morals. This provision ceased to have effect only in 2004, when a new Concordat superseded the previous one.

Article 4 was introduced by the Act which altered the Constitution in 1997. It introduces the right to create private and cooperative schools, which several religious communities can also invoke.

Article 41 of the Constitution, under the general provision on freedom of conscience, religion and form of worship, also considers an important guarantee related to education.

1 https://dre.pt/web/guest/legislacao-consolidada/-/lc/337/202005051737/128002/diploma/indice, last accessed on 5 May 2020.

2 Approved by Decree on 10 of April of 1976, original text available at: http://www.pgdlisboa.pt/leis/lei_busca_art_velho.php?nid=4&artigonum=4A0043&n_versao=1&so_miolo=, last accessed on 5 May 2020.

> Artigo 41.º—Liberdade de consciência, de religião e de culto[3]
> (...)
> 5—É garantida a liberdade de ensino de qualquer religião praticado no âmbito da respetiva confissão, bem como a utilização de meios de comunicação social próprios para o prosseguimento das suas atividades.
> (...)

The first part of article 5 guarantees the freedom to teach any religion within the ambit of the religious communities. This provision ensures the ability to teach within meetings of believers, but also the ability to train clerics of any religion.[4]

7.1 Compulsory Education

Compulsory education in Portugal is provided by both private and public schools. As regards religious education within compulsory education, the Concordat of 1940 referred to above included in its article 21 the Portuguese state's acceptance to include in the curriculum of public schools a mandatory class in Catholic religion and morals. This class was mandatory and an individual option of opting out was given to the parents. The teachers responsible for this class, and for its text and content, had to have previously been approved by the Ecclesiastic Authority in Portugal.[5]

This was the system that operated in public schools until 1987. The right of opting out survived the new Constitution and was transposed into ELD no. 323/83, of 5 July, which regulated the Catholic religion and morals class. This concession, now revoked, was put through a constitutional check. When the judgment was finally published in 1987[6] it determined that the rule requiring a declaration from those who did not want to receive the class was unconstitutional.

Today there is no compulsory religious education in Portugal. However, there is space for religious education in public schools, as permitted by the Religious Freedom Act.

3 https://dre.pt/web/guest/legislacao-consolidada/-/lc/337/202005051250/128000/diploma/indice?q=constitui%C3%A7%C3%A3o+, last accessed on 5 May 2020.

4 Canotilho, Moreira, *Constituição da República*, p. 615.

5 Article XXI of the 1940 Concordat, original text at https://dre.pt/application/file/a/190312, last accessed on 5 May 2020.

6 Judgment of the Portuguese Constitutional Court no. 423/87—original text available at https://dre.pt/application/file/a/499077, last accessed on 5 May 2020.

7.2 Religious Education

The regime of religious education in public schools is the same for all religious communities.

> Artigo 24.º—Ensino religioso nas escolas públicas[7]
> 1—As igrejas e demais comunidades religiosas ou, em sua vez, as organizações representativas dos crentes residentes em território nacional, desde que inscritas, por si, ou conjuntamente, quando para o efeito professem uma única confissão ou acordem num programa comum, podem requerer ao membro do Governo competente em razão da matéria que lhes seja permitido ministrar ensino religioso nas escolas públicas do ensino básico e do ensino secundário que indicarem.
> 2—A educação moral e religiosa é opcional e não alternativa relativamente a qualquer área ou disciplina curricular.
> 3—O funcionamento das aulas de ensino religioso de certa confissão ou programa depende da existência de um número mínimo de alunos, que tenham, pelo encarregado de educação ou por si, sendo maiores de 16 anos, manifestado, expressa e positivamente, o desejo de frequentar a disciplina.
> 4—Os professores a quem incumbe ministrar o ensino religioso não lecionarão cumulativamente aos mesmos alunos outras áreas disciplinares ou de formação, salvo situações devidamente reconhecidas de manifesta dificuldade na aplicação do princípio, e serão nomeados ou contratados, transferidos e excluídos do exercício da docência da disciplina pelo Estado, de acordo com os representantes das igrejas, comunidades ou organizações representativas. Em nenhum caso o ensino será ministrado por quem não seja considerado idóneo pelos respetivos representantes.
> 5—Compete às igrejas e demais comunidades religiosas formar os professores, elaborar os programas e aprovar o material didático, em harmonia com as orientações gerais do sistema do ensino.

Every registered religious community is entitled to ask the Government to be allowed to teach its religion in public schools (number 1). Number 2 goes on to clarify that religious education is facultative, i.e. the students are not obliged to choose any particular religion. They are free to choose not to have any religious

7 https://dre.pt/web/guest/legislacao-consolidada/-/lc/106639383/202005070852/73413239/diploma/indice, last accessed on 5 May 2020.

education in public school in line with the comprehensive view of the freedom of religion—the freedom to choose and change religions or to not have one.

Whether a class is run is dependent on a minimum number of students being allowed by their parents to attend the class or, if the students are 16 or older, themselves clearly stating that they want to attend the class (number 3).

The right of parents to decide on the religious education of their children is also enshrined in the Religious Freedom Act.

> Artigo 11.º—Educação religiosa dos menores[8]
> 1—Os pais têm o direito de educação dos filhos em coerência com as próprias convicções em matéria religiosa, no respeito da integridade moral e física dos filhos e sem prejuízo da saúde destes.
> 2—Os menores, a partir dos 16 anos de idade, têm o direito de realizar por si as escolhas relativas a liberdade de consciência, de religião e de culto.

Article 11 allows parents freely to choose religious education for their children, according to their religion and values, but it imposes a deadline. These decisions are made by the parents only until their minor children turn 16; from this point on the decision on religious education is made by the student him/herself.

Article 24 sets out the rules for teachers—they must teach a class exclusively on a single religion, except in specifically authorised circumstances; they are appointed, hired, transferred and dismissed by the state in conjunction with the representatives of the religious communities (number 4). The curricula are the responsibility of the religious communities and should follow the general guidelines of the educational system (number 5).

ELD no. 55/2018,[9] which sets out the curricula for basic and secondary education and the guiding principles for learning assessment, includes Religious and Moral Education as a subject which must be offered by schools although attendance is optional.

The Portuguese Government's Directorate-General for Education provides information on the curricula of the different religions that are or have been present in public schools since the implementation of the system. Its web-

---

8 https://dre.pt/web/guest/legislacao-consolidada/-/lc/106639383/202005071052/73413225/diploma/indice, last accessed on 5 May 2020.

9 ELD no. 55/2018, 6 of July, the original text of which is available at https://dre.pt/application/file/a/115648908, last accessed on 5 May 2020.

site sets out curricula for the Catholic Church, the Evangelical, Baha'i and Buddhist communities.[10]

In an article in *Público*, a national Portuguese newspaper, in 2015, the representative of the Islamic community explained that the difficulty in introducing a class on Islamic Religion in public schools in Portugal was the minimum number of students that the law requires to exist before a class can begin. This problem is alleviated by the Arabic and Islamic culture classes being taught in mosques every Saturday (a guarantee given by Article 41 (5) of the Portuguese Constitution).[11]

7.3 Private Schools

As previously mentioned, the Portuguese Constitution guarantees the right to set up private and cooperative schools (Article 43 (4)).

The private and cooperative schools' world in Portugal has a strong Catholic presence. However, the Palmela International School[12] stands out as the only school that offers an Islamic religious curriculum in Portugal. It follows the Cambridge curriculum and welcomes students of different beliefs, and the religious curriculum offered is not mandatory (as regulated by ELD no. 55/2018, which also applies to private schools). The school is managed by Palmela's Islamic Community and covers both elementary and secondary education.

10 Available at https://www.dge.mec.pt/educacao-moral-e-religiosa, last accessed on 5 May 2020.

11 Viana, Clara, "Disciplina de Moral e Religião Católica resiste às mudanças curriculares" [Religious Catholic Education Class survives curricular changes], published on 5 April 2015, available at https://www.publico.pt/2015/04/05/sociedade/noticia/moral-e-religiao-catolica-e-uma-disciplina-imune-as-mudancas-curriculares-a-sua-presenca-e-sempre-obrigatoria-1691373, last accessed on 5 May 2020.

12 International School of Palmela, the official website of which is available at https://cip.edu.pt/, last accessed on 5 May 2020.

CHAPTER 8

Further and Higher (Tertiary) Education

As regards higher education, Article 41 (5) of the Portuguese Constitution is the pillar that guarantees freedom to teach any religion.

> Artigo 41.º—Liberdade de consciência, de religião e de culto[1]
> (...)
> 5—É garantida a liberdade de ensino de qualquer religião praticado no âmbito da respetiva confissão, bem como a utilização de meios de comunicação social próprios para o prosseguimento das suas atividades.
> (...)

As stated, the guarantee given by the first part of this provision includes the freedom to teach a religion by means created by the practice of its worship, but also the freedom to train theologians and ministers of religion.[2]

Despite this, higher religious education in Portugal exists only for Catholic theology. There are no institutions promoting or offering training in Islamic religious studies.

1 https://dre.pt/web/guest/legislacao-consolidada/-/lc/337/202005051250/128000/diploma/indice?q=constitui%C3%A7%C3%A3o+, last accessed on 5 May 2020.

2 Canotilho, Moreira, *Constituição da República*, p. 615.

CHAPTER 9

Islamic Chaplaincy in Public Institutions

The right to religious care in public institutions in Portugal is determined by article 13 of the Religious Freedom Act.

> Artigo 13.º—Assistência religiosa em situações especiais[1]
> 1—A qualidade de membro das Forças Armadas, das forças de segurança ou de polícia, a prestação de serviço militar ou de serviço cívico, o internamento em hospitais, asilos, colégios, institutos ou estabelecimentos de saúde, de assistência, de educação ou similares, a detenção em estabelecimento prisional ou outro lugar de detenção não impedem o exercício da liberdade religiosa e, nomeadamente, do direito à assistência religiosa e à prática dos atos de culto.
> 2—As restrições imprescindíveis por razões funcionais ou de segurança só podem ser impostas mediante audiência prévia, sempre que possível, do ministro do culto respetivo.
> 3—O Estado, com respeito pelo princípio da separação e de acordo com o princípio da cooperação, deverá criar as condições adequadas ao exercício da assistência religiosa nas instituições públicas referidas no n.º 1.

First, the norm establishes that the situation of member of the armed forces, security forces or police, military and civilian services, residents in hospitals, nursing homes, colleges, institutes and health care or educational facilities and the like, detainees in prison or other places of detention does not prevent them from exercising religious freedom, and in particular the right to religious care and the practice of acts of worship.[2] We must understand this right as an integral part of the individual dimension of the right to freedom of religion. The state is called on to cooperate with the different religions in the observance of this right (article 13 (3)), with respect for the principle of separation between religious confessions and the state and following the principle of coopera-

1 https://dre.pt/web/guest/legislacao-consolidada/-/lc/106639383/202005071252/73413227/diploma/indice, last accessed on 5 May 2020.

2 Machado, Jónatas, "Religious Assistance in Public Institutions: the Portuguese Case", in *Religious assistance in public institutions—Proceedings of the XXVIIIth Annual Conference, Jurmala, 13–16 October 2016*, Ringolds Balodis and Miguel Rodriguez Blanco (eds.) (Granada: Editorial Comares, 2018), p. 290.

tion.[3] Any limitations needed for functional or safety reasons can be applied only after consultation with and the approval of the Ministry of Religion (article 13 (2)).[4]

During the XVII Constitutional Government (2005–2009)[5] led by the Socialist Party leader and Prime Minister, José Sócrates, regulations on religious assistance were approved to regulate services in the armed and security forces and in the national health and the penitentiary systems.[6]

9.1 Religious Chaplaincy in the Armed and Security Forces

ELD no. 251/2009 was approved on 23 September 2009. It builds on article 13 of the Religious Freedom Act of 2001 and the Concordat of 2004 between Portugal and the Holy See.

The decree guarantees the right to religious care to military, security and civil personnel serving in the armed or security forces (article 2 of ELD no. 251/2009).

> Artigo 3.º—Princípios gerais[7]
> 1—Ao pessoal militar, militarizado, com funções policiais e civil, que exerce funções nas Forças Armadas e nas forças de segurança, independentemente da respetiva confissão, é garantida a assistência religiosa, adiante designada por assistência.
> 2—As igrejas ou comunidades religiosas, legalmente reconhecidas, são livres para prestar assistência aos membros das Forças Armadas e das forças de segurança que a solicitarem, bem como de praticarem os respetivos atos de culto.
> 3—A assistência aos membros das Forças Armadas e das forças de segurança é assegurada através do Serviço de Assistência Religiosa, em respeito pelos princípios consagrados na Lei da Liberdade Religiosa e na Concordata celebrada entre o Estado Português e a Santa Sé.

3 Machado, "Religious Assistance", p. 291.

4 Torres Gutiérrez, *El derecho*, p. 364.

5 With the entry into force of the 1976 Constitution on April 25, executive governments began to be numbered, each receiving, from the first and successively, the corresponding numbering and the designation of constitutional government (*Governo Constitucional*). This is therefore the 17th Executive Cabinet after that date.

6 Machado, "Religious Assistance", p. 292.

7 https://dre.pt/web/guest/pesquisa/-/search/490421/details/normal?q=decreto-lei+251%2F2009, last accessed on 5 May 2020.

4—As igrejas ou comunidades religiosas que pretendam prestar assistência aos membros das Forças Armadas e das forças de segurança devem apresentar, para o efeito, ao membro do Governo competente proposta de celebração de acordo com o Estado, salvo nas situações em que o direito a prestar assistência religiosa se encontre já garantido por força de normas jurídicas específicas.

Article 3 clarifies the general principles on which religious assistance takes place. All the religious communities registered in Portugal are free to provide religious care in the armed and security forces and to practise their worship rites (Article 3 (2)).[8] This important principle, introduced in 2009, is a great innovation towards effective respect for freedom of religion in the armed and security forces. The previous regulation (ELD no. 93/91,[9] revoked by ELD no. 251/2009) only conceived of the possibility of an extension of religious care for non-Catholic religions. That meant that military non-Catholic believers had to ask for an exception to the established Catholic religious care provided by law.

The right to religious care is promoted by the Religious Assistance Service (RAS), in compliance with the principles of the Concordat and the Religious Freedom Act (article 3 (3)). The RAS works by providing spiritual care through a chaplaincy to the three branches of the armed, security and police forces.[10] Its functioning is determined in Chapter II of ELD no. 251/2009.

In general, article 3 (4) establishes the need for an agreement between religious communities and the Government whenever they want to provide religious care for the armed and security forces. "The RAS is an integral part of the structure and hierarchy of the armed and security forces. The chief chaplain and the adjunct chaplains are public servants, and part of the permanent cadre of those forces."[11] The needs of the chaplaincy determine whether the chaplains provide religious care as volunteers or contractors (article 10 of ELD no. 251/2009).

8 Machado, "Religious Assistance", p. 293.

9 The original text is available at https://dre.pt/application/file/a/484353, last accessed on 5 May 2020.

10 Machado, "Religious Assistance", p. 293.

11 Machado, "Religious Assistance", p. 293.

9.2 Religious Chaplaincy in Prison

Executive Legislative Decree no. 252/2009 was also approved on 23 September and it approves the Regulation on Religious and Spiritual Assistance for use in the penitentiary system. Yet again, it builds on article 13 of the Religious Freedom Act and the Concordat of 2004.

All religious communities registered in Portugal are free to provide religious care in the penitentiary system, as long as is requested by the inmate (article 3 (1)). The inmate is guaranteed the right to religious care whatever his/her religion or belief (Article 3 (2)).

Article 4 of the ELD is very clear on who can initiate spiritual and religious assistance. It can be requested by the inmate or by his/her family or people close to him ((1)); it can be initiated by a spiritual assistant from the inmate's religious community, but he/she has to consent to it ((2)); an inmate cannot be forced to receive religious care ((3)).

Article 11 sets out the rights of the inmate regarding religious care.

> Artigo 11.º—Direitos do recluso[12]
> 1—Ao recluso, independentemente da sua confissão, é reconhecido o direito a:
> a) Ter acesso a assistência espiritual e religiosa;
> b) Ser informado por escrito, no momento do ingresso no estabelecimento prisional, dos direitos relativos à assistência durante a reclusão;
> c) Rejeitar a assistência não solicitada;
> d) Ver respeitadas as suas convicções religiosas;
> e) Ser assistido em tempo razoável;
> f) Ser assistido com prioridade em caso de iminência de morte;
> g) Praticar ou participar em atos de culto espiritual ou religioso;
> h) Participar em reuniões privadas com o assistente;
> i) Manter em seu poder publicações de conteúdo espiritual e religioso e objetos pessoais de culto espiritual e religioso, desde que não comprometam a ordem e segurança do estabelecimento prisional e o bem-estar dos demais reclusos;
> j) Beneficiar de uma alimentação, a prestar pelo estabelecimento prisional, na medida do possível, compatível com as suas convicções espirituais e religiosas.

12 https://dre.pt/web/guest/pesquisa/-/search/490415/details/normal?q=decreto-lei+252%2F2009, last accessed on 5 May 2020.

2—Os direitos referidos nas alíneas e) e g) do número anterior podem ser restringidos por razões de disciplina, ordem e segurança do estabelecimento prisional, nos termos da lei e ouvido, sempre que possível, o assistente respetivo.

Prisoners are entitled to access to spiritual and religious care (paragraph a); to be informed in writing of their rights to religious care when they are admitted to prison (paragraph b); to refuse to receive religious care when it was not requested (paragraph c); to be respected in their religious convictions (paragraph d); to receive care within a reasonable time (paragraph e); and with priority if death is imminent (paragraph f); to practise and take part in spiritual acts of religious worship (paragraph g); to participate in private meetings with a religious assistant (paragraph h); to keep in their possession publications with religious content and religious objects, as long as they do not compromise the safety and order of the prison and the wellbeing of other prisoners (paragraph i); whenever possible to have food, to be provided by the prison facility, which accords with their spiritual and religious beliefs (paragraph j).[13]

Religious care in prisons is provided by religious ministers who are chosen by the different religious communities (article 12) and are publicly accredited in accordance with the Religious Freedom Act and registered in the penitentiary system. They can provide their services as contractors or as permanent service providers, depending on the needs of the system.[14]

9.3 Religious Chaplaincy in the National Health Service

Religious care in the National Health Service (NHS) in Portugal is regulated by ELD no. 253/2009.[15] The regulation approves the Regulation of Spiritual and Religious Care (RSRC) in the NHS.

Like the regulations already mentioned, it draws on article 13 of the Religious Freedom Act and the Concordat of 2004. In addition, the approved regulation was also important in putting into practice the National Health Plan 2004–2010 which emphasised the importance of religious and spiritual care in the health care system.[16]

13 Machado, "Religious Assistance", p. 294.

14 Machado, "Religious Assistance", pp. 294–295.

15 The original regulation is available in https://dre.pt/pesquisa/-/search/490426/details/maximized, last accessed on 5 May 2020.

16 Machado, "Religious Assistance", p. 295.

The RSRC applies to every hospital and health facility that admits patients for treatment (article 2). Religious care is based on the principle of universality. That means that all registered religious communities in Portugal are guaranteed the ability freely to provide spiritual and religious care to any patient who wishes it (Article 3 (1)). This principle of universality also means that every patient in those facilities, regardless of his/her faith, is guaranteed access to spiritual and religious care (article 3 (2)).[17]

Throughout the ELD there is a "holistic understanding of spirituality and religion in its diverse dimensions",[18] especially considering the rights of the patients, established in article 12.

> Artigo 12.º—Direitos dos utentes[19]
> Ao utente, independentemente da sua confissão, é reconhecido o direito a:
> a) Aceder ao serviço de assistência espiritual e religiosa;
> b) Ser informado por escrito, no momento da admissão na unidade ou posteriormente, dos direitos relativos à assistência durante o internamento, incluindo o conteúdo do regulamento interno sobre a assistência;
> c) Rejeitar a assistência não solicitada;
> d) Ser assistido em tempo razoável;
> e) Ser assistido com prioridade em caso de iminência de morte;
> f) Praticar atos de culto espiritual e religioso;
> g) Participar em reuniões privadas com o assistente;
> h) Manter em seu poder publicações de conteúdo espiritual e religioso e objetos pessoais de culto espiritual e religioso, desde que não comprometam a funcionalidade do espaço de internamento, a ordem hospitalar, o bem-estar e o repouso dos demais utentes;
> i) Ver respeitadas as suas convicções religiosas;
> j) Optar por uma alimentação que respeite as suas convicções espirituais e religiosas, ainda que tenha que ser providenciada pelo utente.

Regardless of their faith, patients have the right to access spiritual and religious care (paragraph a); to be informed in writing of their right to spiritual and religious care from the moment of admission and later (paragraph b); to refuse care they did not request (paragraph c); to receive assistance within a reasonable

17 Machado, "Religious Assistance", p. 295.
18 Machado, "Religious Assistance", p. 296.
19 https://dre.pt/web/guest/pesquisa/-/search/490426/details/normal?q=decreto-lei+253%2F2009, last accessed on 5 May 2020.

time (paragraph d); to be given priority assistance where death is imminent (paragraph e); to practise acts of spiritual and religious worship (paragraph f); to have private meetings with a religious assistant (paragraph g); to have publications and objects of spiritual and religious content as long as they do not compromise the functionality of the space and the wellbeing and rest of other patients (paragraph h); to have their religious beliefs respected (paragraph i); and to choose a diet that respects their spiritual and religious convictions, even if it has to be provided by the patients themselves (paragraph j).[20]

Spiritual and religious care in the national health service is provided by assistants. These assistants can be either ministers of religion or other individuals who are indicated by the registered religious community as capable of fulfilling the duties listed in article 16 of the RSRC.[21]

In 2011, as an effort to facilitate the implementation of spiritual and religious care to all, the Interreligious Working Group on Health published the *Manual da Assistência Espiritual e Religiosa Hospitalar*—Handbook for Spiritual and Religious Assistance in Hospitals.[22] This handbook lists the religious practices relating to birth, food, sickness and death of 11 religions practised in Portugal. The Working Group is composed of representatives of ten religious communities.

In 2019, an article in a national newspaper complained that the legislation on spiritual and religious care in the National Health Service passed in 2009 had not been fully implemented. The Handbook for Spiritual and Religious Assistance in Hospitals is practically unknown to health professionals and hospital staff. There are still some obstacles to the accreditation of non-Catholic assistants in hospitals, and many believe that the implementation of spiritual and religions care is considered to be more difficult because asking for information on religion at the patient's admission is considered invasive and abusive. Different Portuguese ministers from various religions believe that this should be a standard question that the patient could opt out of answering, arguing that this is the definitive way to respect the patient.[23]

20 Machado, "Religious Assistance", p. 296.

21 "Their duties, the performance of which may depend on specific circumstances, include, amongst others, providing individual spiritual assistance, organising collective worship. Ensuring confidentiality, respecting and not disturbing patients who have not solicited religious care, coordinating with health personnel, complying with hospital administrative rules, keeping the religious neutrality of the State and improving the quality of the service." in Machado, *Religious Assistance*, p. 296.

22 The original version is available in https://www.dgs.pt/em-destaque/manual-de-assistencia-espiritual-e-religiosa-hospitalar-pdf.aspx, last accessed on 5 May 2020.

23 Gomes, João Francisco, "Há um manual sobre a religião nos hospitais, mas (quase) nin-

This is yet another example showing that a discussion of the existence and extent of violations of fundamental rights cannot be complete with just the analysis of the legal framework, but must go further and examine how administrative conduct, by action and inaction, can neutralise constitutional and legal objectives.

---

guém o usa" [There is a handbook about religion in hospitals but nearly (no one) uses it], *Observador*, available at https://observador.pt/especiais/ha-um-manual-sobre-a-religiao-nos-hospitais-mas-quase-ninguem-o-usa/, last accessed on 5 May 2020.

CHAPTER 10

Employment and Social Law

10.1 Employment Law

In the Portuguese legal system, employment law is regulated by the Labour Code with its basis in two key articles in the Portuguese Constitution: Articles 58 and 59. While Article 58 states that everyone has the right to work, Article 59 lists the rights of workers which must be assured by ordinary law.

> Artigo 59.º—Direitos dos trabalhadores[1]
> 1. Todos os trabalhadores, sem distinção de idade, sexo, raça, cidadania, território de origem, religião, convicções políticas ou ideológicas, têm direito:
> a) À retribuição do trabalho, segundo a quantidade, natureza e qualidade, observando-se o princípio de que para trabalho igual salário igual, de forma a garantir uma existência condigna;
> b) A organização do trabalho em condições socialmente dignificantes, de forma a facultar a realização pessoal e a permitir a conciliação da atividade profissional com a vida familiar;
> c) A prestação do trabalho em condições de higiene, segurança e saúde;
> d) Ao repouso e aos lazeres, a um limite máximo da jornada de trabalho, ao descanso semanal e a férias periódicas pagas;
> e) À assistência material, quando involuntariamente se encontrem em situação de desemprego;
> f) A assistência e justa reparação, quando vítimas de acidente de trabalho ou de doença profissional.
> (…)

Article 59 states that every worker, regardless of age, sex, race, citizenship, territory of origin, religion, political or ideological convictions, is entitled to the rights listed in the norm, which include the right to payment for work; to the organisation of work in conditions of social dignity; to rest and leisure time; and to material assistance in the event of involuntary unemployment.

1 https://dre.pt/web/guest/legislacao-consolidada/-/lc/337/202005051450/128022/diploma/indice, last accessed on 5 May 2020.

The Constitution sets the tone for the ordinary law. Thus, Article 24 of the Labour Code provides equal rights regarding access to employment and work.

Artigo 24.º—Direito à igualdade no acesso a emprego e no trabalho[2]
1—O trabalhador ou candidato a emprego tem direito a igualdade de oportunidades e de tratamento no que se refere ao acesso ao emprego, à formação e promoção ou carreira profissionais e às condições de trabalho, não podendo ser privilegiado, beneficiado, prejudicado, privado de qualquer direito ou isento de qualquer dever em razão, nomeadamente, de ascendência, idade, sexo, orientação sexual, identidade de género, estado civil, situação familiar, situação económica, instrução, origem ou condição social, património genético, capacidade de trabalho reduzida, deficiência, doença crónica, nacionalidade, origem étnica ou raça, território de origem, língua, religião, convicções políticas ou ideológicas e filiação sindical, devendo o Estado promover a igualdade de acesso a tais direitos.
(…)

Article 24 (1) states that every worker or applicant for a job has the right to equal opportunities and treatment with regard to access to employment, training, promotion, career or working conditions. There is no tolerance of privileged treatment, advantages, losses or deprivation of rights or duties based on the ancestry, age, sex, sexual orientation, gender identity, civil status, family situation, economic situation, education, origin and social condition, genetic heritage, reduced working capacity, deficiency, chronic disease, nationality, ethnic and racial origin, territory of origin, language, religion, political and ideological convictions and union membership of a worker. The state must promote equality for those rights.

Article 25 clarifies these equal opportunities with the prohibition of discrimination.

Artigo 25.º—Proibição de discriminação[3]
1—O empregador não pode praticar qualquer discriminação, direta ou indireta, em razão nomeadamente dos fatores referidos no n.º 1 do artigo anterior.
(…)

2 https://dre.pt/web/guest/legislacao-consolidada/-/lc/123915628/202005051655/73775342/diploma/indice?q=c%C3%B3digo+do+trabalho, last accessed on 5 May 2020.

3 https://dre.pt/web/guest/legislacao-consolidada/-/lc/123915628/202005051755/73775343/diploma/indice, last accessed on 5 May 2020.

Article 25 obliges the employer not to practise any discrimination, either direct or indirect, specifically on the grounds listed in Article 24 of the Labour Code. In the spirit of laïcism, Portuguese labour law protects against discrimination based on religion. It is also important to refer to Article 55 (4) of the Portuguese Constitution, which establishes that workers' unions are independent of employers, the state, parties and political associations and also religious organisations.

Artigo 55.º—Liberdade sindical[4]
(...)
4. As associações sindicais são independentes do patronato, do Estado, das confissões religiosas, dos partidos e outras associações políticas, devendo a lei estabelecer as garantias adequadas dessa independência, fundamento da unidade das classes trabalhadoras.
(...)

10.2 Religious Needs in Employment and Provision for Days of Rest

As regards religious needs in employment and provisions on days of rest, article 14 of the Religious Freedom Act defines the criteria on which is possible to be excused from work, classes or exams on religious grounds.

Artigo 14.º—Dispensa do trabalho, de aulas e de provas por motivo religioso[5]
1—Os funcionários e agentes do Estado e demais entidades públicas, bem como os trabalhadores em regime de contrato de trabalho, têm o direito de, a seu pedido, suspender o trabalho no dia de descanso semanal, nos dias das festividades e nos períodos horários que lhes sejam prescritos pela confissão que professam, nas seguintes condições:
a) Trabalharem em regime de flexibilidade de horário;
b) Serem membros de igreja ou comunidade religiosa inscrita que enviou no ano anterior ao membro do Governo competente em razão da matéria a indicação dos referidos dias e períodos horários no ano em curso;

4 https://dre.pt/web/guest/legislacao-consolidada/-/lc/337/202004211703/128016/diploma/indice, last accessed on 5 May 2020.

5 https://dre.pt/web/guest/legislacao-consolidada/-/lc/106639383/202004211834/73413228/diploma/indice?p_p_state=maximized, last accessed on 5 May 2020.

> c) Haver compensação integral do respetivo período de trabalho.
> 2—Nas condições previstas na alínea b) do número anterior, são dispensados da frequência das aulas nos dias de semana consagrados ao repouso e culto pelas respetivas confissões religiosas os alunos do ensino público ou privado que as professam, ressalvadas as condições de normal aproveitamento escolar.
> 3—Se a data de prestação de provas de avaliação dos alunos coincidir com o dia dedicado ao repouso ou ao culto pelas respetivas confissões religiosas, poderão essas provas ser prestadas em segunda chamada, ou em nova chamada, em dia em que se não levante a mesma objeção.

The right to be excused from work on the weekly day of rest, festivities and hours that are prescribed by their faith is provided to public officials and private sector workers in article 14 1(1), under three conditions. These workers can be excused from work when they have flexible working hours (paragraph a); when they are members of a church or religious community that has been registered for at least one year (paragraph b); and when they make up for every hour they are excused (paragraph c).

Article 14 (2) and (3) takes into account students from private and public schools who are members of a church or religious community that has been registered for at least a year, excusing them from classes on the appropriate dates and exams and other assessment points as long as this does not affect their educational goals.

Article 14 of the Religious Freedom Act was twice considered in the Portuguese courts. In 2014,[6] a Public Prosecutor brought before the administration an action in which it was claimed that the Public Prosecutor's Office should be required to give a woman leave of absence from important services taking place on Saturday. She was a member of the Seventh-day Adventist Church, whose members must keep Saturday as the day of rest and worship and abstain from secular work. The argument before the Constitutional Court questioned the constitutionality of article 14 (1) (a) of the Religious Freedom Act, for violation of the right to conscience, religion and worship (Article 41 of the Constitution) and violation of the freedom freely to choose one's work (Article 47 of the Constitution). Article 14 (1) (a) states that a worker can be excused on religious grounds only if he/she works flexible hours.

6 Judgement of 15 of July 2014, no. 545/2014, available at http://www.tribunalconstitucional.pt/tc/acordaos/20140545.html, last accessed on 5 May 2020.

In this case, the Constitutional Court upheld the right of the Seventh Day Adventist Public Prosecutor, emphasising that the right to religious freedom, enshrined especially in Article 41 (1) of the Constitution, includes not only a negative component, which guarantees citizens a sphere of autonomy vis-à-vis the state, which implies that it cannot claim the right to impede or prevent the profession and public practice of the religion of a person or community, but also a positive component, which translates into the creation of conditions under which believing citizens can observe their religious duties, allowing them to exercise the right to live according to their faith and to regulate social relations according to their outlook on life and in accordance with the scale of values that results from their professed faith. According to the Court, the Religious Freedom Act, by providing for employees and agents of the state and other public entities, as well as for workers under an employment contract, the opportunity to suspend work under certain conditions on the weekly rest day, on the days of festivities and in the time periods prescribed for them by the confession they profess, does no more than reinforce the right to religious freedom, constitutionally enshrined, in its positive dimension.

The Court stated that there is nothing to prevent flexible schedules being integrated into a flexible working hours regime, in addition to shift work, to which reference has already been made, which allows different fixed hours of arrival and departure for certain groups of staff. The employer's working day continues after the worker's departure, and this allows the concentration of the provision of work into one of the periods of the day, as well as all situations of flexible working hours. Managers will be able to set specific times, whenever other relevant circumstances justify this, which can certainly occur when it comes to the exercise of the right to religious freedom.

In 2014,[7] another case arose in the Labour Court regarding article 14 (1) (a) of the Religious Freedom Act. The worker argued that she had been illegally dismissed from her employment. Doing shift work, she was fired for refusing to work shifts from sundown on Friday to sunset on Saturday based on her religion. This judgment held that the interpretation of article (1) (a) of the Religious Freedom Act should include the possibility of shift work.

The Court thus affirms the existence of a reasonable and proportionate duty, on the part of the private or public employers, to accommodate the practi-

7 Judgment of 15 July 2014, no. 544/2014, available at https://dre.pt/pesquisa-avancada/-/asearch/57301957/details/maximized?emissor=Tribunal+Constitucional&perPage=100&types=JURISPRUDENCIA&search=Pesquisar, last accessed on 5 May 2020.

cal requirements related to the exercise of religious freedom in the context of industrial relations, according to general principles of the weighing of opposing rights and interests, practical agreement, harmonisation and maximum effectiveness.

10.3 Social Law

When discussing social law related to religion it is important to focus on the social protection of ministers of religion in Portugal. Article 16 (3), (4) and (5) of the Religious Freedom Act gives us some understanding of the social treatment of ministers of religion.

> Artigo 16.º—Direitos dos ministros do culto[8]
> (...)
> 3—O exercício do ministério é considerado atividade profissional do ministro do culto quando lhe proporciona meios de sustento, bastando como prova destes para efeito da autorização de residência a ministros do culto estrangeiros a sua garantia pela respetiva igreja ou comunidade religiosa.
> 4—Os ministros do culto das igrejas e demais comunidades religiosas inscritas têm direito às prestações do sistema de segurança social nos termos da lei, sendo obrigatoriamente inscritos pela igreja ou comunidade religiosa a que pertençam, salvo se exercerem por forma secundária a atividade religiosa e o exercício da atividade principal não religiosa determinar a inscrição obrigatória num regime de segurança social.
> 5—Para os efeitos dos dois números anteriores, equiparam-se aos ministros do culto os membros de institutos de vida consagrada e outras pessoas que exercem profissionalmente atividades religiosas e que, como tais, sejam certificadas pela igreja ou comunidade religiosa a que pertençam.

Under the heading "rights of ministers of religion", article 16 (3) provides that this position is considered to be a professional activity when it provides means of sustenance. A guarantee provided by their church or religious community is sufficient for foreign clergy to receive a residence permit in Portugal.

---

8 https://dre.pt/web/guest/legislacao-consolidada/-/lc/106639383/202004221034/73413230/diploma/indice?p_p_state=maximized, last accessed on 5 May 2020.

When it is their primary activity, ministers of religion are entitled to benefits from the social security system. This regime is provided only for ministers of religion who belong to a registered church or religious community. There is no need for ministers of religion to be enrolled in the social security system through their church or religious community if they exercise that profession as a secondary activity and when their primary activity requires that they be enrolled in the social security system (article 16 (4)).

The members of Institutes of Consecrated Life[9] and other people who professionally practise religious activities are equated with ministers of religion and are entitled to the same rights, as long as they are certified by their church or religious community (article 16 (5)).

The Social Security Contributions Code[10] also gives special consideration to members of the clergy. In the chapter on the regime applicable to equivalent situations of dependent work, the first article considers the specific situation of members of churches and religious associations (Article 122 and following).

> Artigo 122.º—Âmbito pessoal[11]
> 1—São abrangidos pelo regime geral, com as especificidades previstas na presente secção, como beneficiários, os membros do clero secular e religioso da Igreja Católica, os membros dos institutos religiosos, das sociedades de vida apostólica e dos institutos seculares da Igreja Católica, bem como os membros do governo das outras igrejas, associações e confissões religiosas legalmente existentes nos termos da lei.
> 2—São ainda abrangidos pelo disposto no número anterior:
> a) Os religiosos e as religiosas que tenham votos ou compromissos públicos e vivam em comunidade ou a ela pertençam;
> b) Os noviços e as noviças, nas condições da parte final da alínea anterior;
> c) Os ministros das confissões não católicas que desempenhem o seu *munus* em atividades de formação próprias daquelas confissões.
> 3—São abrangidos pelo regime geral com as especificidades previstas na presente secção, como contribuintes, as dioceses, os institutos religiosos,

9 An institute of consecrated life is an association of the faithful in the Catholic Church set up and defined by the Canon Law Code (Cannons 573–770) whose members profess the evangelical counsels of chastity, poverty and obedience by vows or other sacred bonds.

10 Law no. 110/2009, 16 September, the original text of which is available at https://dre.pt/web/guest/legislacao-consolidada/-/lc/view?cid=130791222, last accessed on 5 May 2020.

11 https://dre.pt/web/guest/legislacao-consolidada/-/lc/130791222/202005051706/73803418/diploma/indice, last accessed on 5 May 2020.

os institutos seculares, as sociedades da vida apostólica, as fábricas da Igreja e os centros paroquiais da Igreja Católica, bem como as demais associações ou confissões religiosas legalmente existentes, de que dependam ou em que se integrem os beneficiários.

Article 122 sets out the criteria for the scope of the personal application of the general regime with the specificities considered for members of churches and religious associations. This chapter applies to members of the clergy from the Catholic Church, from secular institutions of the Catholic Church and governing members of other churches, associations and religious confessions that are legally registered in Portugal (Article 122 (1)). This also includes religious clergy members that have taken vows to serve the community and are included in it (Article 122 (2) (a)), novices in the same positions (Article 122 (2) (b)), and ministers of non-Catholic confessions who perform their duties in the training and educational activities of their confession (Article 122 (2) (c)).

All religious institutions, associations and organisations in general that employ such people are also considered contributor entities to the social security system (Article 122 (2)).

Artigo 125.º—Âmbito material[12]
1—Sem prejuízo do disposto no número seguinte, os beneficiários referidos no artigo 122.º têm direito à proteção nas eventualidades de invalidez e velhice.
2—Os beneficiários referidos no artigo 122.º podem optar por um âmbito de proteção material que inclui a doença, parentalidade, doenças profissionais, invalidez, velhice e morte.
3—O direito de opção previsto no número anterior é exercido mediante acordo escrito entre a entidade contribuinte e o beneficiário.

Article 125 clarifies the rights to which the beneficiaries defined in Article 122 are entitled. There is protection for disablement and old age (Article 125 (1)). There is also an option to choose protection in the event of disease, parenthood, work-related illness, invalidity, old age and death (Article 125 (2)). This option is pursued by a written agreement between the contributor and the beneficiary (Article 125 (3)).

12 https://dre.pt/web/guest/legislacao-consolidada/-/lc/130791222/202005052006/73803421/diploma/indice, last accessed on 5 May 2020.

CHAPTER 11

Islamic Slaughter and Food Regulation

Religious slaughter is referred to in article 26 of the Religious Freedom Act.

> Artigo 26.º—Abate religioso de animais[1]
> O abate religioso de animais deve respeitar as disposições legais aplicáveis em matéria de proteção dos animais.

This refers to the need to respect any applicable legislation that concerns the protection of animals. This protection was firstly introduced into the Portuguese legal system by ELD no. 28/96, of 2 April.[2] It incorporated the European Directive 39/119/EC[3] on the protection of animals at the time of slaughter or killing.

The original directive is no longer in force. It was repealed by European Regulation no. 1099/2009/EC[4] on the protection of animals at the time of killing. Therefore, Portuguese legislation was updated accordingly through ELD no. 113/2009 of 19 August which executed the Regulation in the Portuguese Legal System.

As such, we should look to the European Regulation for reference about the Religious Slaughter. The general rule determined by Article 4 (1) establishes that "Animals shall only be killed after stunning in accordance with the methods and specific requirements related to the application of those methods (…)".

However, article 4 (4) contributes with an important exemption of the general rule in situations where methods of slaughter prescribed by religious rites, and therefore stunning is not permitted.

> Artigo 4.º—Métodos de atordoamento[5]
> 1—Os animais só podem ser mortos após atordoamento efetuado em conformidade com os métodos e requisitos específicos relacionados com a

1 https://dre.pt/web/guest/legislacao-consolidada/-/lc/106639383/202005071452/73413241/diploma/indice, last accessed on 5 May 2020.

2 The original text is available https://dre.pt/web/guest/pesquisa/-/search/548449/details/normal?q=Decreto-Lei+28%2F96, last accessed on 8 October 2020

3 The original text is available at https://eur-lex.europa.eu/legal-content/EN/ALL/?uri=celex%3A31993L0119, last accessed on 5 May 2020.

4 https://eur-lex.europa.eu/legal-content/EN/TXT/?uri=CELEX:02009R1099-20191214

5 English version available in https://eur-lex.europa.eu/legal-content/EN/TXT/?uri=CELEX:02009R1099-20191214, last accessed on 8 October 2020.

> aplicação desses métodos especificados no anexo I. A perda de consciência e sensibilidade é mantida até à morte do animal.
> Os métodos referidos no anexo I que não resultem em morte instantânea (adiante referidos como «atordoamento simples») são seguidos, o mais rapidamente possível, por um processo que assegure a morte, tal como sangria, mielotomia, electrocussão ou exposição prolongada a anóxia.
> (...)
> 4—Os requisitos previstos no n.º 1 não se aplicam aos animais que são objecto dos métodos especiais de abate requeridos por determinados ritos religiosos, desde que o abate seja efetuado num matadouro.

The previous Portuguese legislation established a similar regime regarding the exception of animal stunning when religious rites apply to the slaughter. This update, from a Directive to a Regulation, at European level, is – as practice in the European Union – a way to harmonize legislation throughout all member states.

CHAPTER 12

Islamic Goods and Services

Islamic goods, such as Halal food, are verified in Portugal by the Halal Institute of Portugal.[1] This organisation analyses, monitors, inspects and certifies halal products. It certifies that animals for human consumption are slaughtered according to the criteria defined by Sunni jurisprudence.

In parallel, the Portuguese Institute for Quality has produced quality standard 4559:2018. This quality requirement must be respected by any company that wants to produce Halal food. It sets out the criteria for the production, storage and transport of Halal meat.[2]

1 Instituto Halal de Portugal, https://halal.pt/en/ihp/, last accessed on 5 May 2020.

2 NP 4559:2008, Certification Term No. 42/2018, 2018-02-08, *Instituto Português de Qualidade*, http://www1.ipq.pt/PT/Pages/Homepage.aspx, last accessed on 5 May 2020.

CHAPTER 13

Islamic Dress

In Portugal, there is no restriction relating to dress. However, the identity document, the "Citizen Card", includes restrictions regarding the identification photograph that can conflict with traditional religious attire.

Act no. 7/2007 of 2 May[1]—last amended by Act no. 32/2017—regulates the procedure of issuing the "Citizen Card". This directive is regulated by decree no. 286/2017[2] of the Presidency of the Cabinet and the Ministry of Justice. In annexe II to this decree, it is stated that the identification image of the citizen should comply with the recommendations of the "ICAONTWG: Biometrics deployment of machine-readable travel documents, technical report, version 2.0".[3]

These recommendations include a restriction on the wearing of head clothing that can potentially hinder the recognition of the person, both by human and biometrical/technological reading.[4] The norm is an internationally accepted directive, based on security grounds, which can affect Islamic community members.

1 A consolidated version of the original text is available at https://dre.pt/web/guest/pesquisa/-/search/518073/details/normal?p_p_auth=1Mgl0oN3, last accessed on 5 May 2020.

2 The original text is available at https://dre.pt/application/file/a/108225930, last accessed on 5 May 2020.

3 The original text is available at https://www.icao.int/Meetings/TAG-MRTD/Documents/Tag-Mrtd-17/TagMrtd17_WP016.pdf, last accessed on 5 May 2020.

4 ICAONTWG: Biometrics deployment of machine readable travel documents, technical report, version 2.0, p. 27.

CHAPTER 14

Criminal Law

The Portuguese Criminal Code was approved by Executive Legislative Decree no. 400/82 of 23 September 1982.[1] It has gone through several amendments during the years, the last by Act no. 58/2020, of 31 August 2020[2] with a view to aligning the rules of the Portuguese legal system with the Council of Europe's Convention against Human Trafficking.

There is no specific provision regarding the protection of a particular religion such as Islam. However, the Criminal Code contains some important protections regarding religion and religious feelings.

Analysing the chapter on crimes against life we can find that the crime of murder is aggravated when it includes an element of religious hatred. The crime of murder defined in Article 131 determines that killing another person is punishable by a prison sentence of from eight to 16 years.

> Artigo 132.º—Homicídio qualificado[3]
> 1—Se a morte for produzida em circunstâncias que revelem especial censurabilidade ou perversidade, o agente é punido com pena de prisão de doze a vinte e cinco anos.
> 2—É suscetível de revelar a especial censurabilidade ou perversidade a que se refere o número anterior, entre outras, a circunstância de o agente:
> (…)
> f) Ser determinado por ódio racial, religioso, político ou gerado pela cor, origem étnica ou nacional, pelo sexo, pela orientação sexual ou pela identidade de género da vítima;
> (…)
> l) Praticar o facto contra membro de órgão de soberania, do Conselho de Estado, Representante da República, magistrado, membro de órgão do governo próprio das regiões autónomas, Provedor de Justiça, membro de órgão das autarquias locais ou de serviço ou organismo que exerça

1 An updated and consolidated version is available at https://dre.pt/web/guest/legislacao-consolidada/-/lc/34437675/view?q=c%C3%B3digo+penal, last accessed on 5 May 2020.

2 The original text is available at https://dre.pt/web/guest/pesquisa/-/search/141382321/details/maximized, last accessed on 8 October 2020.

3 https://dre.pt/web/guest/legislacao-consolidada/-/lc/124532375/202005051720/73759128/diploma/indice?q=codigo+penal, last accessed on 5 May 2020.

autoridade pública, comandante de força pública, jurado, testemunha, advogado, solicitador, agente de execução, administrador judicial, todos os que exerçam funções no âmbito de procedimentos de resolução extrajudicial de conflitos, agente das forças ou serviços de segurança, funcionário público, civil ou militar, agente de força pública ou cidadão encarregado de serviço público, docente, examinador ou membro de comunidade escolar, ministro de culto religioso, jornalista, ou juiz ou árbitro desportivo sob a jurisdição das federações desportivas, no exercício das suas funções ou por causa delas;

Article 132 lists the circumstances that are especially reprehensible or wicked in which the perpetrator ought to receive a prison sentence of from 12 to 25 years (the maximum penalty in Portugal).

Taking into account the protection of religious freedom, Article 132 (2) (f) considers it to be aggravation whenever the perpetrator is motivated by racial hatred, religious hatred, political hatred, ethnic or national hatred or gender or sexual orientation hatred in the commission of the crime.

There is also an important provision in Article 132 (2) (l) which governs aggravation based on the victim's position in society. This contains a list of positions which includes ministers of religion. So whenever the victim happens to be a minister of religion the legislation considers the crime especially reprehensible or wicked, and this entails punishment of up to a maximum of 25 years in prison.

In the chapter that lists crimes against property, we can emphasise the special protection of Article 204. While Article 203 considers the crime of theft punishable by a maximum of three years in prison or a fine, Article 204 considers the circumstances in which the theft is considered aggravated.

Artigo 204.º—Furto qualificado[4]
1—Quem furtar coisa móvel ou animal alheios:
(…)
c) Afeta ao culto religioso ou à veneração da memória dos mortos e que se encontre em lugar destinado ao culto ou em cemitério;
(…)
é punido com pena de prisão de dois a oito anos.

4 https://dre.pt/web/guest/legislacao-consolidada/-/lc/124532375/202005051920/73759221/diploma/indice last accessed on 5 May 2020.

In the specific case of article 204 (1) (c) whoever steals movable property or an animal that belongs to others, intended for religious rite or prayers in memory of a deceased or which is found in a cemetery or a place of worship is punishable by two to four years imprisonment.

Criminal damage—which consists of someone damaging, disfiguring or rendering unusable the property of others—under Article 212 can lead to a penalty of up to three years in prison or a fine, and the following legal provision deals with the situation where the penalty should be increased.

> Artigo 213.º[5]
> Dano qualificado
> 1—Quem destruir, no todo ou em parte, danificar, desfigurar ou tornar não utilizável:
> (…)
> e) Coisa ou animal alheios afetos ao culto religioso ou à veneração da memória dos mortos e que se encontre em lugar destinado ao culto ou em cemitério;
> é punido com pena de prisão até cinco anos ou com pena de multa até 600 dias.

Article 213 (1) (e) deals with an aggravated situation, in which the author of the crime is punishable by up to five years imprisonment or fine of up to 600 days.[6] Whenever an object is damaged, disfigured or rendered unusable and the purpose of this object is religious worship, or use in prayers in memory of the deceased or the object is situated in a cemetery or a place of worship, the crime of aggravated damage is committed.

Further in the Criminal Code there is a section on crimes against religious feelings. This section comprises Articles 251 and 252.

> Artigo 251.º—Ultraje por motivo de crença religiosa[7]
> 1—Quem publicamente ofender outra pessoa ou dela escarnecer em razão da sua crença ou função religiosa, por forma adequada a

5 https://dre.pt/web/guest/legislacao-consolidada/-/lc/124532375/202005052120/73759230/diploma/indice, last accessed on 5 May 2020.

6 In the Portuguese criminal system, fines are measured in days. The judge attributes a value to each day, based on the socio-economic position of the perpetrator and then decides on the number of days to be paid, given the severity of the crime, amongst other considerations.

7 https://dre.pt/web/guest/legislacao-consolidada/-/lc/124532375/202005052320/73759277/diploma/indice, last accessed on 5 May 2020.

perturbar a paz pública, é punido com pena de prisão até 1 ano ou com pena de multa até 120 dias.
2—Na mesma pena incorre quem profanar lugar ou objeto de culto ou de veneração religiosa, por forma adequada a perturbar a paz pública.

Anyone who publicly offends someone on the grounds of their belief or religious function, thus causing a breach of the public peace, is punishable by imprisonment for up to one year or a fine of up to 120 days,[8] The same sanction applies to anyone who desecrates a place or object of religious worship.

Artigo 252.º—Impedimento, perturbação ou ultraje a ato de culto[9]
Quem:
a) Por meio de violência ou de ameaça com mal importante impedir ou perturbar o exercício legítimo do culto de religião; ou
b) Publicamente vilipendiar ato de culto de religião ou dele escarnecer;
é punido com pena de prisão até 1 ano ou com pena de multa até 120 dias.

Article 252 lays down a penalty of up to one year's imprisonment or a fine of up to 120 days[10] for those who violently or by means of a serious threat obstruct or disrupt legitimate religious worship (Article 152 (a)) and those who publicly vilify or belittle an act of religious worship (Article 152 (b)).

8 See above footnote 6.

9 https://dre.pt/web/guest/legislacao-consolidada/-/lc/124532375/202005060020/73759278/diploma/indice, last accessed on 5 May 2020.

10 See above footnote 6.

CHAPTER 15

Family Law

The Portuguese Constitution in Article 67 protects the family as a fundamental element of society. This legal provision introduces the right to the protection of the family from society and from the state. The state must provide conditions conducive to the personal accomplishment of every member of the family.

Article 36 of the Portuguese Constitution sets out the basic principles of family law.

> Artigo 36.º—Família, casamento e filiação[1]
> 1. Todos têm o direito de constituir família e de contrair casamento em condições de plena igualdade.
> 2. A lei regula os requisitos e os efeitos do casamento e da sua dissolução, por morte ou divórcio, independentemente da forma de celebração.
> 3. Os cônjuges têm iguais direitos e deveres quanto à capacidade civil e política e à manutenção e educação dos filhos.
> 4. Os filhos nascidos fora do casamento não podem, por esse motivo, ser objeto de qualquer discriminação e a lei ou as repartições oficiais não podem usar designações discriminatórias relativas à filiação.
> 5. Os pais têm o direito e o dever de educação e manutenção dos filhos.
> 6. Os filhos não podem ser separados dos pais, salvo quando estes não cumpram os seus deveres fundamentais para com eles e sempre mediante decisão judicial.
> 7. A adoção é regulada e protegida nos termos da lei, a qual deve estabelecer formas céleres para a respetiva tramitação.

The Constitution enshrines the right to form a family and to marry without any discrimination (Article 36 (1)). It also devolves to the ordinary law the task of laying down the preconditions for marriage, its effects and the effects of its dissolution by death or divorce (Article 36 (2)). It then prescribes that there is equality between spouses as regards their rights and duties, civil and political capacity and the bringing up and education of the children (Article 36 (3)); this equality principle is also extended to the children, who cannot be discriminated against for having being born outside marriage (Article 36 (4)).

1 https://dre.pt/web/guest/legislacao-consolidada/-/lc/337/202005051650/127995/diploma/indice, last accessed on 5 May 2020.

This provision also makes clear that parents have a right and obligation to educate and bring up their children (Article 36 (5)), who cannot be separated from their parents unless there is a failure to fulfil parental duties and, even then, only with the intervention of a court (Article 36 (6)). Adoption is also constitutionally protected, which implies that the state should provide funds for the process (Article 36 (7)).

The major provisions on family law are included in Book IV of the Civil Code.

15.1 Private International Law

Private international law assumes an important role in family relationships. If the family includes members of more than one nationality or is distributed across different countries, private international law helps us to define what law applies to each situation.

When there is a concurrence of different rules, the Portuguese Civil Code clarifies for different situations which law should prevail.

With reference to family relationships, these clarification rules begin in Article 49 of the Civil Code.

> Artigo 49.º—Capacidade para contrair casamento ou celebrar convenções antenupciais[2]
> A capacidade para contrair casamento ou celebrar a convenção antenupcial é regulada, em relação a cada nubente, pela respetiva lei pessoal, à qual compete ainda definir o regime da falta e dos vícios da vontade dos contraentes.

Article 49 provides that the capacity to enter into a marriage or to celebrate a prenuptial agreement is defined by the couple's personal law.[3] When it comes to the celebration, its form is determined by the law in which the act is observed (Article 50). The rules that apply to filiation and parenthood are set out in Articles 56 to 61.

Given the specificity of Islam and the acceptance of polygamous marriages by many legal systems based on Sharia law, it is important to determine how the Portuguese legal system welcomes these legal situations. The principle of

2 https://dre.pt/web/guest/legislacao-consolidada/-/lc/123928118/202005051730/73747142/diploma/indice?q=c%C3%B3digo+civil, last accessed on 5 May 2020.

3 The personal law is the law of the couple's nationality, as determined by Article 31 (1) of the Civil Code.

monogamy is part of public order in Portugal and in other European countries. Therefore, in principle, any polygamous marriage should not be recognised by the Portuguese legal system, even if it was legally celebrated abroad.[4] This rejection of foreign rules that are against public order is set out in Article 22 of the Civil Code.[5] However, if polygamous marriage had no legal recognition in Portugal, an individual could legitimately marry in another European country and there would be no way to require a divorce or annulment of such second marriage. So, polygamous marriage is recognised as a marriage impediment (Article 1601 (c)) and to be the basis for a divorce or annulment action. There are also voices being raised for the acceptance of the effects of polygamous marriage as a basis for the need for the payment of maintenance or for a wife to be certified as an heir together with others.[6]

The Portuguese Civil Code sets out, in Article 23, how foreign law should be interpreted—within its own system and in accordance with its interpretative rules. The only exception to the application of foreign law is Article 22 on public order.

Artigo 22.º—Ordem pública[7]
1. Não são aplicáveis os preceitos da lei estrangeira indicados pela norma de conflitos, quando essa aplicação envolva ofensa dos princípios fundamentais da ordem pública internacional do Estado português.
2. São aplicáveis, neste caso, as normas mais apropriadas da legislação estrangeira competente ou, subsidiariamente, as regras do direito interno português.

15.2 Marriage and Divorce

As regards marriage there are some important characteristics that should be kept in mind. First, the Portuguese system has a dual system of marriage. The Civil Code assumes the legal validity of both Catholic and civil marriage. Even though the effects of each are the same, the possibility of annulment of the

4 Pinheiro, Jorge Duarte, "Poligamia e uniões paralelas", *in Estudos de Direito da Família e da Crianças*, (Lisboa: AAFDL, 2015), p. 196.
5 The original text is available at https://dre.pt/web/guest/legislacao-consolidada/-/lc/123928118/202005041706/73747109/diploma/indice, last accessed on 5 May 2020.
6 Pinheiro, "Poligamia", p. 196.
7 https://dre.pt/web/guest/legislacao-consolidada/-/lc/123928118/202005042107/73747109/diploma/indice, last accessed on 5 May 2020.

Catholic marriage by the clerical court is considered.[8] This is a direct effect of the international obligations that the Portuguese state assumed in the Concordat with the Holy See.

With the Religious Freedom Act of 2001, it became possible for a civil marriage to be celebrated in the context of a religious celebration. This deserves to be emphasised, as sometimes there is some confusion. Portuguese law does not recognise Christian marriage in general or Catholic Christian in particular, nor does it recognise Jewish, Islamic or Hindu marriage. It recognises only civil marriage, the legal effects of which are regulated by the rules of the Civil Code. Thus, for example, even if the ceremony is Catholic or Islamic, the legal regime must always be that of the Civil Code. If a religious community allows polygamy, it will not be accepted by the Portuguese legal system. If another confession permits marriage to underage girls, that too will not be allowed in Portugal. If a religious community permits no means of dissolution of a marriage, that rule will also not be considered legally binding in Portugal. The aforementioned possibility of annulment of Catholic marriage by the ecclesiastical authority is a minor limitation of the generally valid principle of exclusivity and prevalence of the effects of civil marriage. The freedom of individual and collective religion cannot be invoked to justify a marriage regime which seriously threatens people's rights to dignity, freedom, equality, and physical and psychological integrity.

Artigo 19.º—Casamento na forma religiosa[9]
1—São reconhecidos efeitos civis ao casamento celebrado por forma religiosa perante o ministro do culto de uma igreja ou comunidade religiosa radicada no País. O ministro do culto deverá ter a nacionalidade portuguesa ou, sendo estrangeiro, não nacional de Estado membro da União Europeia, ter autorização de residência temporária ou permanente em Portugal.
2—Aqueles que pretendam contrair casamento por forma religiosa deverão declará-lo, pessoalmente ou por intermédio de procurador, no requerimento de instauração do respetivo processo de publicações na conservatória do registo civil competente, indicando o ministro do culto creden-

8 Artigo 1625.º (Competência dos tribunais eclesiásticos)—O conhecimento das causas respeitantes à nulidade do casamento católico e à dispensa do casamento rato e não consumado é reservado aos tribunais e às repartições eclesiásticas competentes.—Original text available in https://dre.pt/web/guest/legislacao-consolidada/-/lc/123928118/202005031137/73749076/diploma/indice?q=C%C3%B3digo+Civil, last accessed on 5 May 2020.

9 https://dre.pt/web/guest/legislacao-consolidada/-/lc/106639383/202005071652/73413233/diploma/indice, last accessed on 5 May 2020.

ciado para o ato. A declaração para casamento pode ainda ser prestada pelo ministro do culto, mediante requerimento por si assinado.
3—Autorizada a realização do casamento, o conservador passa o certificado para casamento, nos termos dos artigos 146.º e 147.º do Código do Registo Civil, com as necessárias adaptações. O certificado não é passado sem que o conservador se tenha assegurado de que os nubentes têm conhecimento dos artigos 1577.º, 1600.º, 1671.º e 1672.º do Código Civil. O certificado deve conter menção deste facto, bem como do nome e da credenciação do ministro do culto. O certificado é remetido oficiosamente ao ministro do culto, a quem são igualmente comunicados os impedimentos de conhecimento superveniente.
4—É indispensável para a celebração do casamento a presença:
a) Dos contraentes, ou de um deles e do procurador do outro;
b) Do ministro do culto, devidamente credenciado;
c) De duas testemunhas.
5—Logo após a celebração do casamento, o ministro do culto lavra assento em duplicado no livro de registo da igreja ou da comunidade religiosa e envia à conservatória competente, dentro do prazo de três dias, o duplicado do assento, a fim de ser transcrito no livro de assentos de casamento.
6—O conservador deve efetuar a transcrição do duplicado dentro do prazo de dois dias e comunicá-la ao ministro do culto até ao termo do dia imediato àquele em que foi feita.

The celebration of marriage in a religious form is allowed to every settled religious community in Portugal. The minister who performs the ceremony must be of Portuguese citizenship or the holder of a residence permit, either temporary or permanent, when not a citizen of a European Union member state (article 19 (1)).

The preliminaries to marriage (Article 1610 and following of the Civil Code[10]) that are mandatory for the celebration of a civil marriage are also mandatory in this situation. They can be initiated by the engaged couple or by the accredited minister who will perform the ceremony (article 19 (2)). After the celebration, the act is registered in the Civil Registry (article 19 (5)). The only limitation established by law about the way the wedding can be performed is the attendance of the couple getting married (one of them can be represented), the minister of religion and two witnesses (article 19 (4)).

10 This section of the Civil Code is available at https://dre.pt/web/guest/legislacao-consolidada/-/lc/123928118/202005031152/73749055/diploma/indice?q=c%C3%B3digo+civil, last accessed on 5 May 2020.

The engaged couple should also be aware of the provisions of Articles 1671 and 1672 of the Civil Code (article 19 (3)).

Artigo 1671.º—Igualdade dos cônjuges[11]
1. O casamento baseia-se na igualdade de direitos e deveres dos cônjuges.
2. A direção da família pertence a ambos os cônjuges, que devem acordar sobre a orientação da vida em comum tendo em conta o bem da família e os interesses um do outro.

Equality between the spouses is clearly introduced in Article 1671 as one of the personal legal effects of marriage. This equality takes effect as regards both the rights and obligations that may come with the celebration of marriage (article 1671 (1)).

Decisions relating to the household should be made by both spouses, taking into account the well-being of the family and the interests of both (article 1671 (2)).

Artigo 1672.º—Deveres dos cônjuges[12]
Os cônjuges estão reciprocamente vinculados pelos deveres de respeito, fidelidade, coabitação, cooperação e assistência.

As a result of their marriage, the spouses have a duty of mutual respect, fidelity, cohabitation, cooperation and assistance.

The Portuguese legal system does not accept polygamous marriages. Article 1601, which lists the absolute impediments to marriage, emphasises this prohibition when it states that a marriage cannot take place when there is a previous marriage, either Catholic or civil, that has not yet been dissolved (Article 1601 (c)).[13] Criminal law also punishes bigamy in Article 247 of the Criminal Code,[14] laying down a penalty of up to two years' imprisonment or a fine of 240

11 https://dre.pt/web/guest/legislacao-consolidada/-/lc/123928118/202005051930/73749143/diploma/indice, last accessed on 5 May 2020.

12 https://dre.pt/web/guest/legislacao-consolidada/-/lc/123928118/202005052030/73749144/diploma/indice, last accessed on 5 May 2020.

13 The original text available in https://dre.pt/web/guest/legislacao-consolidada/-/lc/123928118/202005041511/73749046/diploma/indice?q=c%C3%B3digo+civil, last accessed on 5 May 2020.

14 The original text available in https://dre.pt/web/guest/legislacao-consolidada/-/lc/124532375/202005041512/73759272/diploma/indice?q=c%C3%B3digo+penal, last accessed on 5 May 2020.

days[15] for those who marry even though they are already married and for those who marry someone who is already married. In the Portuguese legal system bigamy is considered a crime against the family.

Divorce is allowed for every form of marriage considered in the civil law, as set out in Article 36 (2) of the Constitution. Even when the marriage is celebrated in a religious ceremony it is recognised as a civil marriage by Portuguese law and can therefore be dissolved as such. The legal framework for divorce is set out beginning in Article 1773 of the Civil Code.[16]

15.3 Children

Specifically relating to children there are two points worth referring to in our context. As mentioned above[17] the Portuguese Constitution enshrines the principle of equality between children born within a marriage and those outside it (Article 36 (4)). It also does not allow discrimination based on gender—all children must be treated equally by both parents (Article 36 (5)).[18]

As a Contracting State of the Hague Conference on Private International Law Convention on Jurisdiction, Applicable Law, Recognition, Enforcement and Co-operation in Respect of Parental Responsibility and Measures for the Protection of Children (1996), Portugal[19] cooperates in cases of children located in other countries by implementing alternative solutions to adoption such as the Islamic solution of *kafala*.

> Article 33[20]
> (1) If an authority having jurisdiction under Articles 5 to 10 contemplates the placement of the child in a foster family or institutional care, or the

15 See footnote 6 from Chapter 14.

16 The original text is available at https://dre.pt/web/guest/legislacao-consolidada/-/lc/123928118/202005041547/73749263/diploma/indice?q=c%C3%B3digo+civil, last accessed on 5 May 2020.

17 See above—15. Family Law

18 Article 36 of the Portuguese Constitution, the original text of which is available at https://dre.pt/web/guest/legislacao-consolidada/-/lc/337/202005042123/127995/diploma/indice?q=constitui%C3%A7%C3%A3o, last accessed on 5 May 2020.

19 Decree no. 52/2008, of 13 November approves the accession of Portugal to the Convention, and its original text is available at https://dre.pt/web/guest/pesquisa/-/search/439855/details/normal?q=kafala.

20 https://hcch.net/en/instruments/conventions/full-text/?cid=70#ch4, last accessed on 5 May 2020.

provision of care by kafala or an analogous institution, and if such placement or such provision of care is to take place in another Contracting State, it shall first consult with the Central Authority or other competent authority of the latter State. To that effect it shall transmit a report on the child together with the reasons for the proposed placement or provision of care.
(2) The decision on the placement or provision of care may be made in the requesting State only if the Central Authority or other competent authority of the requested State has consented to the placement or provision of care, taking into account the child's best interests.

As a State Party to the UN's Convention on the Rights of the Child, Portugal makes sure that all children receive alternative protection. Although it is set out in the list of alternative protection methods, the institution of kafala is not specifically included in the Portuguese legal system.

Artigo 20.º[21]
1—A criança temporária ou definitivamente privada do seu ambiente familiar ou que, no seu interesse superior, não possa ser deixada em tal ambiente tem direito à proteção e assistência especiais do Estado.
2—Os Estados Partes asseguram a tais crianças uma proteção alternativa, nos termos da sua legislação nacional.
3. A proteção alternativa pode incluir, entre outras, a forma de colocação familiar, a kafala do direito islâmico, a adoção ou, no caso de tal se mostrar necessário, a colocação em estabelecimentos adequados de assistência às crianças. Ao considerar tais soluções, importa atender devidamente à necessidade de assegurar continuidade à educação da criança, bem como à sua origem étnica, religiosa, cultural e linguística.

When alternative protection is given to children, continuity in the child's upbringing and ethnic, religious, cultural and linguistic background is taken into account.

21 The original text is: "ARTICLE 20 1—A child temporarily or permanently deprived of his or her family environment, or in whose own best interests cannot be allowed to remain in that environment, shall be entitled to special protection and assistance provided by the State. 2—States Parties shall in accordance with their national laws ensure alternative care for such a child. 3—Such care could include, inter alia, foster placement, kafalah of Islamic law, adoption, or, if necessary, placement in suitable institutions for the care of children. When considering solutions, due regard shall be paid to the desirability of continuity in a child's upbringing and to the child's ethnic, religious, cultural and linguistic background.

Bibliography

Argiolas, Davide, *A Responsabilidade Civil das Entidades Religiosas*, (Lisboa: Petrony Editora, 2017).

Assembleia da República, Separação do Estado das Igrejas (1911), available at https://www.parlamento.pt/Parlamento/Paginas/Separacao-Estado-Igrejas.aspx, last accessed on 5 May 2020.

Canotilho, J.J. Gomes, *Direito Constitucional e a Teoria da Constituição* (Coimbra: Almedina, 2003).

Canotilho, J.J. Gomes, Moreira, Vital, *Constituição da República Portuguesa: anotada, Volume I* (Coimbra: Coimbra Editora, 2014).

Canotilho, José Joaquim Gomes, Machado, Jónatas, "Metódica Multinível: Acordos Internacionais do Estado Português com Comunidades Religiosas", *Revista de Legislação e Jurisprudência*, 3963 (2010), pp. 254–269.

Carvalho, Rita Maria Cristovam Cipriano Almeida, *A Concordata de Salazar Portugal-Santa Sé 1940*, (Lisboa: FCSH, UNL, 2009) pp. 7 and ff.

Gomes, João Francisco, "Há um manual sobre a religião nos hospitais, mas (quase) ninguém o usa" [There is a handbook about religion in hospitals but nearly (no one) uses it], *Observador*, available in https://observador.pt/especiais/ha-um-manual-sobre-a-religiao-nos-hospitais-mas-quase-ninguem-o-usa/, last accessed on 5 May 2020.

Lopes, Manuela Baptista, "A Liberdade Religiosa em Portugal, a(s) constituição (ões) e o tribunal constitucional", in *Estudos em Homenagem ao Conselheiro Presidente Rui Moura Ramos, Volume I—Direito Constitucional, Direito Constitucional Europeu, Direito Europeu*, Maria Lúcia Amaral (org.) (Coimbra: Almedina, 2016).

Machado, Jónatas E.M., *Liberdade Religiosa numa comunidade constitucional inclusiva dos direitos da verdade aos direitos dos cidadãos* (Coimbra: Coimbra Editora, 1996).

Machado, Jónatas, "Religious Assistance in Public Institutions: the Portuguese Case", in, *Religious assistance in public institutions—Proceedings of the XXVIIIth Annual Conference, Jurmala, 13–16 October 2016*, Ringolds Balodis, Miguel Rodriguez Blanco (ed.) (Granada: Editorial Comares, 2018).

Machado, Jónatas, *O Regime Concordatário entre a "Libertas Ecclesiae" e a Liberdade Religiosa—Liberdade de Religião ou liberdade da Igreja?* (Coimbra: Coimbra Editora, 1993).

Ministry of Justice, *Proposta de Lei apresentada à Assembleia da República*, (Lisbon: Ministério da Justiça, 1999).

Miranda, Jorge, Medeiros, Rui, *Constituição Portuguesa Anotada, Volume I*, (Coimbra: Coimbra Editora, 2010).

Pinheiro, Jorge Duarte, "Poligamia e uniões paralelas", *in Estudos de Direito da Família e da Crianças*, (Lisboa: AAFDL, 2015).

Index

Printed in the United States
By Bookmasters